Is Fairtrade Fair?

Is Fairtrade Fair?

Elisabeth Valiente-Riedl
University of Sydney, Australia

First published 2013 by
PALGRAVE MACMILLAN

Palgrave Macmillan in the UK is an imprint of Macmillan Publishers Limited, registered in England, company number 785998, of Houndmills, Basingstoke, Hampshire RG21 6XS.

Palgrave Macmillan in the US is a division of St Martin's Press LLC, 175 Fifth Avenue, New York, NY 10010.

Palgrave Macmillan is the global academic imprint of the above companies and has companies and representatives throughout the world.

Palgrave® and Macmillan® are registered trademarks in the United States, the United Kingdom, Europe and other countries.

ISBN 978–0–230–30815–2

This book is printed on paper suitable for recycling and made from fully managed and sustained forest sources. Logging, pulping and manufacturing processes are expected to conform to the environmental regulations of the country of origin.

A catalogue record for this book is available from the British Library.

A catalog record for this book is available from the Library of Congress.

10 9 8 7 6 5 4 3 2 1
22 21 20 19 18 17 16 15 14 13

Printed and bound in Great Britain by
CPI Antony Rowe, Chippenham and Eastbourne

To Daniel, Maya – 'Mein Sonnenschein' – and Rosa.

Contents

List of Figures and Tables

Figures

Tables

Acknowledgements

There are countless people to thank – people who have given so generously of their time and have made invaluable contributions to this research. For their mentoring, I would like to thank Dr Tim Anderson, Dr Joy Paton, Professor Frank Stilwell, Professor David Goodman, Professor Louise Chappell and Associate Professor Danielle Celermajer. To the many people who have shared their time and knowledge with me over the years, I also offer my thanks. In no particular order: Jessica Eitelberg, Robert Heijdacker, Bert Beekman, Peter Baker, Sarah Obraitis, Dawn Ward, Eugene Karagodin, Jos Harmsen, David Rosenberg, Guillermo Denaux, Roel Vaessen, Mick Wheeler, Pablo Dubois, Shailen Singh, Jon and Mary Jogiyo, Bernard Goma, Brendan Ellis, Gary Ellis, Willie Mapa, Joseph Warai, Henry Ame, Moses Alu, Yanny Guman; to my friends at the Bismarck Ramu Group (BRG); and to all the smallholder coffee growers who shared their stories and who demonstrate a level of courage that will always inspire me.

For their research assistance, I would like to acknowledge the support of Tonya Roberts; Alex Matthews-Peat; Kelly Nims, Ph.D.; and Nadia Jones, Esq. I would also like to thank the team at Palgrave who supported this book from the original concept to print, in particular, Eleanor Davey-Corrigan, Virginia Thorp, Keri Dickens and Mritunjai Sahai.

I would also like to express my gratitude to my support network through this process: Daniel Valiente-Riedl, Rosmarie Riedl, Susanne Riedl, Regina Eberle Riedl and Josef Riedl. A very special thanks is owed to Rosa Riedl who provided her unwavering support through all aspects of this process.

List of Acronyms

4C Association	Common Code for the Coffee Community
AA	AccountAbility
ADB	Asian Development Bank
AFTF	Asia Fair Trade Forum
ANC	African National Congress
AoA	Agreement on Agriculture
APEC	Asia-Pacific Economic Cooperation
ATOs	Alternative Trade Organisations
C.A.F.E. Practices	Coffee and Farmer Equity Practices
CC	Cooperative Coffees
CI	Consumers International
COFTA	Cooperation for Fair Trade in Africa
CPL	Cafédirect Producers Ltd
CSR	Corporate Social Responsibility
CSU	Cooperative Societies Unit
ECF	European Coffee Federations
EFTA	European Fair Trade Association
ETI	Ethical Trade Initiative
EU	European Union
FINE	Four key international fair trade associations, representing labelling organisations and ATOs – FLO, WFTO, NEWS! and EFTA.
FLO	Fairtrade Labelling Organisations International
FLO-Cert	Fairtrade certification organisation
FLO e.V	Internal body of FLO responsible for standard-setting
FTF	Fair Trade Federation
FTOs	Fair Trade Organisations

FTUSA	Fair Trade USA
GATT	General Agreement on Tariffs and Trade
GDP	Gross Domestic Product
GNI	Gross National Income
GPG	Global Public Good
GSP	General System of Preferences
HOAC	Smallholder coffee producers' cooperative
ICAO	International Cooperative Agricultural Organisation
ICAs	International Coffee Agreements
ICFTU	International Confederation of Free Trade Unions now renamed as ITUC
ICO	International Coffee Organisation
IFAT	International Federation for Alternative Trade
IFOAM	International Federation of Organic Agriculture Movements
ILO	International Labour Organisation
ILRF	International Labour Rights Fund
IMF	International Monetary Fund
ITC	International Trade Centre
ITO	International Trade Organisation
LDCs	Least Developed Countries
MNC	Multinational Corporation
NAP	Network of Asian Producers
NEWS!	Network of European Worldshops!
NCC	National Consumer Council
NGO	Non-Government Organisations
(N)LI's	(National) Labelling Initiatives
OCS	Office of the Cooperative Societies
OECD	Organisation for Economic Co-operation and Development
PNG	Papua New Guinea
PPP	Producer Partnership Programme
PSRU	Producer Services and Relations Unit
PSU	Pricing Subunit

SAPs	Structural Adjustment Programmes
SAR	Self-Assessment Reports
SC	Standards Committee
SMBC	Smithsonian Migratory Bird Certification
SSU	Standards Subunit
SU	Standards Unit
TOR	Terms of Reference
TRIMS	Trade Related Investment Measures
TRIPS	Trade Related Intellectual Property Rights
UK	United Kingdom
UN	United Nations
UNCTAD	United Nations Conference on Trade and Development
US/USA	United States of America
USTR	United States Trade Representative
WBCSD	World Business Council for Sustainable Development
WFTOs	World Fair Trade Organisations
WTO	World Trade Organization

1
Introduction

In recent years we have witnessed an upsurge in the debate over international trading rules and practices, with advocates of 'fair trade' both actively critiquing the integrity of a 'free trade' system and promoting alternative strategies for global exchange. This has emerged with increasing intensity through awareness of the important relationship between global trade and development. One of the strengths of this debate is that it has questioned the integrity of the dominant economic orthodoxy, in terms of both free trade principles and practices: does 'free' trade support a process of development? Yet this is perhaps the one question that fails to be understood or tested with reference to fair trade arguments that advocate alternative trade practices: does 'fair' trade support a process of development? While there appears little room for doubt on the first question, can consumers feel certain that their 'Fair Trade' purchases will resolve the ills of the global trading system?

With its origins in the activities of non-governmental organisations (NGOs), Fair Trade emerged as the 'war cry' of a social movement based in developed countries, championing the plight of marginalised producers in developing countries. Conceived as an 'alternative trade' movement, through the activities of dedicated Alternative Trade Organisations (ATOs), it has since reinvented itself as Fair Trade and is setting a clear challenge to the dominant global free trade architecture. However, the authenticity of Fair Trade is also increasingly challenged, and in particular critique is levelled at the introduction of the Fairtrade labelling strategy and its controversial partnership with conventional businesses. 'Fairtrade' – one word – is a registered trademark for a product label, which vouches for the conditions of trade associated with any products bearing the label. It does not belong to any one country, producer group or company. It is also not to be confused with 'Fair Trade' – two words (capitalised, in contrast to 'fair trade' which refers to the concept) – an umbrella term for a myriad of philosophies and practices that promise to bring fairness to global trade. While the latter offers a seemingly open and live debate, within which a singular definition of fairness in trade remains elusive, the former offers a very specific and arguably one-dimensional understanding. Between the two we move from the very broad to the extremely narrow, and yet the narrow product mark is what most modern-day consumers will know as fair trade and which has served to become the most popular and accessible model of fair trade to date. Yet can you put a 'price' on fairness – or essentially – can you put a label on it?

Fair Trade has certainly evolved beyond its traditional mantra of 'alternative trade', characterised by ethical businesses, ethical supply chains and the small markets they operated in. Today, Fairtrade invites the traditional corporate 'bad boys', like McDonald's, Wal-Mart and Starbucks, to feature ethical brands in their menu of products. For consumers, this begs the question: does the purchase of a Fairtrade coffee at Starbucks balance out the availability of conventionally traded blends on the menu board? Essentially, are our 'voting' dollars best spent on Fairtrade or better invested in alternative forms of lobbying to ensure change also takes place in the conventional market? For the marginalised producers in developing countries, which Fairtrade aims to assist, it will be important to establish whether Fairtrade provides opportunities to improve livelihoods beyond those offered in the conventional market. For participating producers, this is likely a relatively simple answer of 'yes'. Yet the scale of commodity traps in the global market may well eclipse Fairtrade's capacity to fix, controversially leaving ethical consumers with an ethical market to invest their energies in, while the bulk of producers continue to suffer the conditions that afflict the conventional market. This is exemplified in the case of Fairtrade's most mature commodity market – coffee.

Is free trade 'fair'? Coffee producers in crisis

At the turn of the twenty-first century, coffee – one of the most heavily traded agricultural commodities – was thrown into arguably the worst crisis it had faced in 100 years when prices fell to their 'lowest levels in 30 years, and to 100 year lows if adjusted for inflation' (Lewin, Giovannucci and Varangis, 2004, p. 1). The severity of this crisis not only 'plunged' millions of producers into poverty, but it also captured the attention of global civil society organisations, with them the corporations they accused of exploitation, and perhaps for the first time it captured the attention of the humble coffee drinker. NGOs were relentless in their outrage, with Oxfam claiming that for '25 million coffee producers around the world . . . [t]he coffee crisis is becoming a development disaster whose impact will be felt for a long time' (Gresser and Tickell, 2002, p. 6). Prompted by civil society groups, consumers began to understand that the importance of a cup of coffee extends beyond the pleasure of taste or of the café culture enjoyed in the predominantly developed countries of the world. In fact, the importance of coffee in trade lies less in the sustenance it gives the coffee addicts that drink it, but more importantly in the sustenance it should, yet fails to offer the producers that grow it.

Lewin, Giovannucci and Varangis (2004, p. 1) estimate that 'between 17 and 20 million families are directly involved in coffee production'. Most of this production occurs in the so-called developing countries and is undertaken by 'smallholder' coffee producers, who work 'small' plots of land, typically less than five hectares, to grow their crop. Considering the enormous magnitude of global coffee production, not only in terms of the scale of production but also in terms of the scale of production by *marginalised producers*, it is not surprising that the coffee trade is perceived as vital to development across the globe. In fact, the poor performance of coffee and other tropical commodities, which are also characterised by extreme volatility in prices, are causally linked to global poverty and has led Robbins (2003, p. 3) to conclude that '[t]he collapse of tropical commodity prices represents the most formidable obstacle to efforts to lift huge numbers of people out of poverty'.

The poverty associated with smallholder coffee production stands in stark contrast to the income it raises for traders in the consuming markets, and the value it holds for consumers in these markets. Coffee is a highly valuable commodity in the global economy. For the period following World War II it was second only to oil as the most valuable traded commodity, a position it only surrendered in the mid-1990s (Daviron and Ponte, 2005, p. 50). Predominantly consumed in the 'north' or wealthier economies, and predominantly produced in the tropical 'south' or developing economies,[1] why is it that the consumer value of this commodity does not translate into higher incomes for coffee producers? After all, as most coffee addicts will tell you, it is a commodity they simply cannot do without. It is this contradiction, the fact that low coffee incomes have impoverished millions of smallholder coffee producers while consumers continue to depend on, and enjoy, sipping their espressos or lattes, which has set a challenge to the perceived integrity of current free trade arrangements. This contradiction, this inequity in the distribution of wealth, firmly raises the fundamental question: are current 'free' trade arrangements 'fair'? The answer to this question appears to be a resounding 'No'! Yet can Fairtrade offer the 'coffee fix' it promises?

The chapters

This book will navigate the various concerns outlined previously in a number of ways. It begins with an examination of the conceptual debates around fairness in trade and then turns to an evaluation of the performance of the free trade regime. Fairtrade, including its history in the alternative trade movement, is then examined in-depth across four chapters. The book concludes with an evaluation of the rise of ethical consumption in an effort to contextualise the potential value of ethical initiatives like Fairtrade.

Chapter 2 will outline a conceptual framework for identifying and understanding different arguments for fairness in trade. These approaches are broadly categorised as a 'freedom', a 'rights linkage', a 'value distribution', an 'ecological sustainability' and a 'business accountability' approach to fair trade. The 'value distribution' approach, which is at the heart of this research, is associated with fair trade models that prioritise enhancing producer participation in, and benefit from, trade. Through its focus on value distribution, this category of fair trade is particularly relevant for an analysis of the capacity of Fairtrade labelling to enhance the livelihoods of marginalised producers.

Chapter 3 assesses the operation of the current free trade regime and the historic shift from regulation to trade liberalisation in agriculture. It evaluates value distribution trends in agricultural trade, focusing in on the coffee case study. This chapter functions in two ways. First, it provides a context for the development of alternative trade practices that are currently operating within the trading superstructure and that typically aim to redress perceived failures within it. Second, the results obtained in this chapter provide 'control' data and observations, against which the relative results obtained for Fairtrade practices can be measured and understood.

Chapter 4, while acknowledging the important links between Fair Trade through ATO networks and Fairtrade labelling, especially in terms of shared history, shared principles and some overlap in activities (particularly in coffee), explores some of the important differences between these two models. The process and scope of inclusion of conventional businesses in the Fairtrade labelling model is the key point of departure from ATO Fair Trade. In this chapter, the argument is put forward that mainstreaming is made possible through the device of the Fairtrade 'label', which signifies the *product assurance* given in Fairtrade labelling, as opposed to the *business assurance* given in ATO Fair Trade. To evaluate the integrity of product assurance in Fairtrade, considering that there is no guarantee of the integrity of participating conventional businesses, Chapter 5 will evaluate the governance structure and standards that underpin the Fairtrade labelling model. Questions regarding multi-stakeholder participation in Fairtrade labelling, as well as the burden of responsibilities conferred on traders and producers by Fairtrade standards, will be examined.

Chapter 6 provides an examination of the opportunities for smallholder coffee producers to *access* Fairtrade labelling. This chapter recognises that an evaluation of the *impact* of Fairtrade on smallholder coffee producers (in Chapter 7) is meaningless without first understanding how relevant (i.e. *accessible*) this market is. It quickly becomes apparent that only a limited number of smallholder producers (who, as required by the rules of Fairtrade, are mobilised through collective organisational structures) presently have access to the Fairtrade market, a situation that is unlikely to improve dramatically in the future. If we examine the *terms of access*, we begin to build a profile of the type of producer that is eligible to join. This profile does not typically meet the self-professed mission of Fairtrade to enlist the most marginalised producers.

Chapter 7 looks holistically at the impact of Fairtrade by bringing together a range of the arguments examined in previous chapters, as well as new analysis and data on impacts. In particular, data on Fairtrade incomes for coffee producers, through Fairtrade minimum prices and premiums, is evaluated. This chapter also includes an examination of the opportunities offered by cooperative production and trade networks, which are also important, although not *exclusive*, features of the Fairtrade model.

Finally, Chapter 8 contextualises Fairtrade labelling within the broader ethical consumption movement. Here the analysis turns to the potential value of ethical consumption more generally, as a means to trace the potential trajectory and value of ethical initiatives like Fairtrade. Despite the constraints of Fairtrade's niche market, this chapter suggests that as part of a broader shift towards transformation in consumption practices, ethical initiatives like Fairtrade may have a greater potential impact on market transformation in the future. At the same time, it questions the participation of corporate actors in ethical trading schemes, and the scope for ethical consumption to transform the behaviour of commercial businesses.

2
What's Fair about Fair Trade

Ownership of fair trade is claimed across a diverse range of ideologies and practices. Fair trade has even been used by some free trade advocates to represent their own methods and achievements. Consequently, affiliation with the fair trade banner does not necessarily exclude free trade strategies as might be expected. A key challenge is to ensure that the distinction between fairness arguments is understood. Some posit a conventional trade liberalisation model while others advocate alternative trade practices and their networks (defined as distinct from the dominant free trade paradigm). This understanding is fundamental to identifying and evaluating not only free trade strategies and practices but also to identifying and evaluating applied alternatives to conventional trading practices.

There is an evident theoretical gap in trade discourse which the conceptual approach developed here seeks to engage. It identifies five broad fair trade arguments based on different understandings of the concept of fairness in trade. These five approaches to fairness in trade are: freedom, rights linkage, value distribution, ecological sustainability and business accountability. There are significant overlaps within and between these conceptual categories. However, the framework makes it possible to identify key differences in fairness values for trade. Further it identifies mechanisms for fair conduct in trade, which vary in terms of their alignment with the free market model. In particular, a value distribution approach to fairness in trade – associated with traditional alternative trade and also Fairtrade labelling practices – focuses on enhancing the opportunities of marginalised producers.

The argument will be put forward that the opportunities offered to marginalised producers in value distribution Fair Trade models must be understood comparatively against the performance of free markets.

Even so, the legitimacy of this approach also needs to be advanced against self-defined principles and measures assessing the capacities of associated models to create enhanced opportunities, relative to those already offered in conventional trade. Too often attacking the perceived weaknesses of a competing approach or model defends the merits of an individual approach and of associated models. Later in this chapter, the idea will be put forward that the merit of an individual approach needs to be tested on the integrity of its application and its performance against independent measures.

Conceptual approach to understanding fair trade arguments

McDonagh (2002, p. 643) claims that '[N]o universally accepted, authoritative definition of fair trade exists.' It is certainly difficult to arrive at a universally accepted definition of fair trade. If we were to discuss the concept of free trade, it would be cloaked in the authority of neoclassical theory of economics and would be defined in practice as the elimination of market barriers facilitating an open trade regime. Fair trade, however, is less easy to define, as its foundations are not rooted in a distinct or cohesive body of theory.

Robert Freer (1938, p. 303) took the approach that it is only possible to decipher the 'intended meaning of such labels as . . . "fair trade"' with reference 'to the context in which they are used'. Certainly, there are a variety of different contexts in which the words fair trade are applied. Fair trade is traditionally associated with the commerce of dedicated alternative trade organisations (ATOs), which actively trade in handicrafts and food products with the aim of supporting marginalised producers in the developing world (see discussion in Chapter 4). Today it is perhaps more commonly identified with 'Fairtrade' certification, of which certified coffee remains the most popular product in a growing range of goods labelled Fairtrade. However, it has also been used in many other contexts, including its use by free trade proponents endorsing trade liberalisation, advocates of organic production practices and labour rights campaigners. In fact, by employing a conceptual approach to fair trade, distinguishing between different propositions for what is fair in trade, it is possible to identify a range of both explicit and implicit fair trade arguments. There is after all, no limit to the range of possible opinions, approaches and models for defining and implementing fairness in trade.

Table 2.1 reproduces the basic structure of this conceptual approach to fair trade, which is based on respective arguments for fairness in

Table 2.1 Approaches to fairness in trade

Approach	Fairness defined as	Examples of associated mechanisms	Key supporters
Freedom	*Free trade* Equal opportunity to participate in markets	Current trade regime under the World Trade Organization (WTO)	US, WTO, orthodox economists
	Freer trade Improve market access through more equitable liberalisation	Advance liberalisation, especially in traditionally neglected areas like agriculture	Australia, WTO Secretariat
Rights Linkage	*Industry protection* To prevent labour rights abuse in a third country	State action – block imports to protect domestic industries	Western manufacturers and manufacturing trade unions
	Social clause Link trade liberalisation to compliance with basic labour rights	Link fundamental conventions of International Labour Organisation (ILO) to regional and international trade treaties (with trade sanctions for non-compliance)	The International Confederation of Free Trade Unions (ICFTU), International Labour Rights Fund (ILRF)
	Civil solidarity Coordinated solidarity sanctions or preferences	Action at the request of democratic organisations – emphasising assistance (occasional coordinated sanctions)	African National Congress (ANC) (anti-apartheid campaign)
	General System of Preferences Low tariffs for good LDCs	Unilateral trade preferences based on rights, democratic performance	US, EU, Australia
Value Distribution	*Supply and price management* International price leverage through the producer/consumer cartel	Regulate volatile commodity prices through quotas in production and floor prices in case of overproduction	International Coffee Organisation (ICO, a coffee cartel) – historical formation of cartels overseen by the UN on the authority of the Havana Charter

	Cooperative trade networks Remove monopoly to better reward small producers and consumers	Worker-owned and -operated entities, democratic participation, preference for cooperative-to-cooperative trade	International Cooperative Alliance, cooperatives
	ATOs Remove monopoly to better reward small producers	ATOs (often non-profit) trade directly with marginalised producers in developing countries (mostly handicrafts and food products)	Oxfam, World Fair Trade Organisation (WFTO)
	Fairtrade labelling Mainstream marketing of Fairtrade through corporate participation	Product differentiation through labelling of products, where participating corporations/ATOs have agreed to share value with small producers and hired labour for those certified products	Fairtrade Labelling Organisations International (FLO), WFTO
Ecological Sustainability	*International trade treaties* Attempt to gain international agreement on environmental standards and targets	Kyoto Protocol	Environmental groups
	Sustainability certifications Allowing corporations to demonstrate environmental performance and consumers to choose sustainable products	Sustainability certifications such as for organics	Some businesses, consumers and activist groups
Business Accountability	*Corporate code of practice* Based on an understanding of corporate social responsibility, businesses develop voluntary codes of practice at the company or industry level	UN Global Compact, Ethical Trade Initiative (ETI, based in the UK) and individual corporate initiatives	Unions, civil society, corporations and government

(continued)

Table 2.1 Continued

Approach	Fairness defined as	Examples of associated mechanisms	Key supporters
	Sustainability certifications A certification driven by business interests to create means for responsible sourcing, implementation of base standards and proof of compliance	Utz Certified in coffee based on EurepGap protocol for certification	Some major coffee buyers and roasters, European Coffee Federation (ECF)

Source: The categories of Freedom, Rights Linkage and Value Distribution are adapted from Anderson and Riedl (2006).

trade. The inclusion of a freedom approach to fair trade, even though this approach is usually identified with free trade, is based on the premise that both the language and definition of fair trade remain malleable and have been adopted broadly in the debate over international trade. The rights linkage approach recognises strategies, which promote the realisation of universal rights and standards comprising labour rights, human rights and, in some cases, environmental standards. The value distribution category is specifically concerned with the distribution of value between wealthier and developing countries through the international trading system. An argument for ecological sustainability recognises the ecology as a finite resource, which in order to be protected, needs to be valued in market transactions. Finally, the category of business accountability refers to the argument that corporations have a fundamental impact on sustainable development, and as such a primary responsibility in fostering sustainable development, a responsibility to which they should be held accountable. Each of these categories will be examined in turn, though noting at the outset that the examples provided to clarify each category are not exhaustive and that, while it is useful to examine them individually for conceptual clarity, there are important and often significant overlaps across the principles and strategies attributed to each category respectively.

Freedom as fairness

For trade liberalisation advocates, fairness is achieved through freedom of exchange. The promise is that a free trade system, by providing an open market that establishes property rights and the right of equitable access and opportunities, will achieve economic growth, which in turn will trickle down for broader social benefits. This is reflected in a joint position adopted by the International Monetary Fund (IMF), the World Bank and the WTO (2003), which claims that trade directly, but also indirectly through its capacity to bring investments which spur income growth and create jobs, 'help[s] raise people out of poverty and make[s] economies more resilient to shocks'. While the explicit promise is for freedom of exchange to promote economic growth, neoclassical economists (and their representative institutions) draw upon an implied principle of fairness, the realisation of which is directly linked to freedom of exchange. This is evident where practices that compromise the integrity of free trade are perceived as unfair or protectionist, thus reinforcing the implication that fairness in trade is achieved through free trade.

Essentially, the linkage of free and fair trade is argued on two important levels. First, trade liberalisation advocates advance principles of freedom of exchange, as synonymous with principles of fairness for trade and development. Second, by making a distinction between the theory and practice of free trade, some advocates argue that while current trade practices may be flawed, the principles of freedom of exchange are not, thereby warranting a 'commitment to freer trade' (Bhagwati, 1995, p. 745). There are two key problems with this logic. First, there is an assumption that freedom will produce fairness, and yet there is no explanation of how this will occur. Welford, Meaton and Young (2003, p. 3) note that while 'the international economic order is fixated on growth: the quantitative increase in national output per year . . . growth [quantitative process] and development [qualitative process] are different', thereby claiming that the assumption that growth will promote development is seriously flawed. Second, free trade advocates draw on a level of circular reasoning where, if free trade policies fail to produce social benefits or fair trade, then the solution is freer trade. In this argument, free trade advocates often hold the persistence of protectionist or unfair trade accountable. Thus it is also important to understand trade liberalisationists' arguments against this so-called protectionism or unfair trade and to examine the legitimacy of this type of argument as a scapegoat for underperformance (this is discussed later in the chapter).

Linking rights to fairness

Rights advocates of fair trade seek to link universal rights or standards to conduct in international trade. Fairness in trade from this perspective emphasises fair competition. The key claim is that competition should uphold fundamental social and political values as well as base environmental standards, and not purely economic goals. Further, competition based on low or lowering standards in any of these areas is tantamount to unfair trade. Instead, a fair trade approach promoting a level playing field requires a strategy for the harmonisation of rights and standards.

A concern with establishing and enforcing universal rights is particularly evident in the push for a social clause, which rights advocates seek to attach to WTO trade treaties. The aim is to integrate global rights and standards, such as those contained in the conventions of the ILO, into the rules and enforcement structure of the international trade regime. Through the device of a social clause, countries could place restrictions on imports that do not comply with specified minimum international labour standards (Bagwell and Staiger, 2001, p. 519). The ICFTU proposed that the review and implementation of rights embodied in a trade-linked social clause could be monitored through the establishment of a joint WTO/ILO Advisory Body (LeQuesne, 1996, p. 56). This would ensure that the rules of international trade reflect a universal right to qualitative and sustainable environmental, social, economic and political standards. Effectively, the intention is to abolish competition on the basis that it contributes to low, or lowered labour standards. However, the push for a social clause – which was particularly fervent in the 1990s – has not succeeded to date.[1]

Another important rights linkage model for fair trade is the proposal for trade-linked civil or international sanctions in the case of rights violations. In this model 'environmentalists and labour rights activists may advocate trade sanctions as a means of inducing recalcitrant governments and/or firms to meet a given set of labour or environmental standards' (Howse and Trebilcock, 1996, pp. 62–3). There is already some precedent for this. Historically, trade sanctions have been applied by a number of states in response to perceived human rights violations such as apartheid in South Africa and genocide in the former Yugoslavia (Howse and Trebilcock, 1996, p. 63). Further, under current trade rules it is possible for countries to formally discriminate against goods produced by prison labour (Hamilton, 2001, p. 62).

Finally, the General System of Preferences (GSP), which was first proposed by Raúl Prebisch (the first Secretary-General of the United Nations Conference on Trade and Development – UNCTAD) in 1964 (and integrated into the multilateral trade regime in 1968), recognises a right to development through trade (UNCTAD, 2012). The GSP provides legal recourse for the preferential treatment of developing countries with an aim to 'increase their export earning; to promote their industrialisation; and to accelerate their rates of economic growth' (UNCTAD, 2012). Unilaterally countries can choose to apply reduced or zero tariff rates for selected products from developing countries. Broadly this scheme is concerned with ensuring that trade facilitates, and indeed promotes, a universal right to development.

The fairness of value distribution

A value distribution argument for fair trade is concerned with the distribution of value through global exchange networks and with the governance structures that support patterns of distribution. The objective in this category of fair trade is to develop strategies for value redistribution, whereby relationships of exchange are restructured to ensure that developing economies have equal access and opportunities in the global trading system. Before the advent of trade liberalisation, a value distribution strategy was exemplified in the supply (and thereby) price management strategy of international producer/consumer cartels, most famously in coffee through the regulatory measures enacted under the auspices of the ICO. This organisation administered the provisions of the International Coffee Agreements (ICAs), which included economic provisions until 1989 when these provisions lost the support of key member countries (see Chapter 3). However, value distribution strategies have an even longer history in alternative trade networks, including the (often shared) pathways of cooperatives and ATOs.

Young (2003, p. 4) explains that historically fair trade can 'be traced back to the late 19th century cooperative movements in Europe, with their desire to create an integrated cooperative economy from the producer to the retailer'. Indeed, cooperative trade is distinguished as a trade model which seeks to empower a whole chain of actors, particularly producers and consumers, both through the democratic structure of individual cooperatives, and the explicit preference for trade with other cooperatives (creating holistic cooperative trade networks; see Chapter 7). As such it is not surprising that the cooperative model serves as an important feature in alternative trade networks, especially in the preference of ATOs to work with cooperative producer organisations, but also in some cases through the adoption of the cooperative structure by ATOs at the consuming end of the chain.

ATOs serve as pioneers of Fair Trade, as a concept and market model focused on producer empowerment. The goal is very much to assist developing economies through trade, not aid. For ATOs who identify with this strategy, value distribution is the key problem with current trade practices. Oxfam (2002, p. 22) insists that the wealth generated by trade 'is not being shared on an equitable basis' and indeed, that 'income differences between rich and poor countries, already obscene, are widening, and undermining the potential for poverty reduction'. Essentially, a value distribution argument for fair trade asserts that current trade practices and associated governance structures fail to promote and support conditions necessary for development.

Udomkit and Winnett (2002, p. 45) note that such Fair Trade movements are primarily 'concern[ed] for producers and their communities'. They claim that Fair Trade (here, the authors are interested in trade that operates according to Fair Trade principles mandated by Fairtrade labelling organisations) can be characterised according to 'at least two dimensions: financial and social' (Udomkit and Winnett, 2002, p. 45). The first dimension emphasises 'fair prices and a margin for producers for investment in order to sustain business and livelihoods'; the second dimension features 'direct purchasing from producers, a transparent trading system, equal partnership and exclusive contracts'. Additionally, they propose that a third 'environmental dimension' can be included (Udomkit and Winnett, 2002, p. 45). This conceptualisation of Fair Trade emphasises the economic, social and environmental integrity of trade by focusing on the nature of relationships of exchange. Essentially, Fair Trade is required to yield both economic and social benefits.

Ecological sustainability arguments for fairness

Broadly speaking, ecological sustainability arguments recognise the importance of protecting finite ecological resources and promoting sound ecological management in production and trade practices. This means that protection of the environment, in production (for agro-commodities particularly) but also through exchange, is the primary driver behind ecological sustainability models. This is not to say that such models are incompatible with market mechanisms, or that they do not also include other sustainability objectives (especially worker's rights in sustainability certifications). It simply means that ecological sustainability models, including international regulatory initiatives and sustainability certifications, are motivated primarily by ecological concerns, even while these are increasingly understood as also fundamental to industry survival.

The organic movement largely pioneered the application of ecological sustainability concerns in the production and trade of agricultural products. Today organics has evolved into a rigorous certification system across a large range of agricultural products, with organic standards set and governed by the International Federation of Organic Agriculture Movements (IFOAM). Further administration by national or regional members of IFOAM sees these standards applied in individual countries. Organics is also unique among certification systems in that 'organic certification standards are often set or regulated by governments', including EU, US and Japanese regulations (Consumers International and the International Institute for Environment and Development, 2005, p. 24), adding an additional level of governance to that already assumed by the organic certification bodies. While today the organic movement consists of a broad sustainability agenda, comprising the principles of 'health', 'care', and 'fairness' - in addition to the principle of 'ecology' (IFOAM, 2009) – these elements are also understood to be interlinked, whereby improved ecological practices are best served by the application of all of these principles. For example, for the principle of 'health' the aim is to 'sustain and enhance the health of soil, plant, animal, human and planet *as one and indivisible'* (IFOAM, 2009; emphasis added).

Equating fairness with business accountability

Increasingly the fate of economic enterprise, ecology, social values and development processes around the world are understood to be irrevocably bound. In arguments for business accountability, many commercial businesses recognise they not only have important impacts on the broader community (including economic, environmental and social impacts) but they also have a responsibility to work towards fostering sustainable development in their business practices and throughout their supply chains. The extent to which such concern is driven by consumer expectations is of course debated. Irrespective of this, the development of corporate codes of practice, ranging from company- to industry-wide codes as well as sustainability certifications, see businesses increasingly platform their role as important drivers of sustainable development.

The underlying logic that underpins the development of corporate codes of practice is that of corporate social responsibility (CSR), a now common catchcry in the corporate world. Holme and Watts (2000) in a publication by the World Business Council for Sustainable Development (WBCSD) note that 'a universally accepted definition of CSR has yet to emerge'. Nevertheless, they provide a working definition of CSR, first crafted in an earlier report of 1998, which provides an indication of the approach the global business community has with regard to the social responsibilities of businesses (Holme and Watts, 2000, p. 8). They define CSR as 'the continuing commitment by business to behave ethically and contribute to economic development while improving the quality of life of the workforce and their families as well as the local community and society at large' (Holme and Watts, 2000, p. 8). As part of their CSR commitments, companies are encouraged 'to articulate their own core values and codes of conduct' (Holme and Watts, 2000, p. 4). While businesses are no strangers to developing budgets, economic strategies, market research and the like, corporate codes of conduct and social audits are among the many manifestations of an alleged emerging corporate conscience. Yet CSR commitments are as likely to be driven by public relations motivations, as they are (if at all) by a growing social conscience.

Holme and Watts (2000, p. 2) explain that 'CSR is increasingly viewed, not only as making good business sense but also contributing to the long-term prosperity of companies and ultimately [their] survival'. This observation surely throws into question the rising social conscience of business, if the argument that the call for social responsibility is also tied to business survival instincts is accurate. In fact, it is likely that the new age CSR image of business is as intrinsic an economic strategy as a financial budget. As much as corporations recognise their responsibilities, they are equally, if not more motivated, by concerns about their reputation and thus their consumer base. Whether business accountability is tied more to economic or social motives, the outcome is clear; CSR is becoming an important part of business values and practices.

An example of CSR as adopted by businesses engaged in international trade is the ETI based in the UK. Broadly, 'ethical trade', like 'fair trade', can refer to a range of business practices and trade arrangements; but the ETI (2012a) applies a very specific understanding of ethical trade, whereby it refers to the application of base labour standards in a company's supply chain. Arguably, this model could fit very well into the rights linkage category of fairness arguments, not least because this particular initiative comprises a tripartite membership of stakeholders, including trade union representatives as well as corporate (retailers and suppliers) and non-government organisation (NGO) stakeholders (ETI 2012a). Moreover, this model bears an important resemblance to a rights linkage model because of its commitment to labour rights, with the 'ETI Base Code'... founded on the conventions of the International Labour Organisation' (ETI, 2012b). The point of difference, however, is that such multi-stakeholder codes, and other ethical trade codes of conduct on either the company or industry level, uniquely position businesses as accountable and best equipped to handle sustainability issues in their supply chains, typically without external (e.g. third-party or regulatory) interference. The ETI, like other ethical trade initiatives, is voluntary, and can be distinguished as an approach to fairness whereby business not only recognises its responsibility to sustainable development, but also seeks to self-regulate on these issues (as opposed to having external regulations or monitoring imposed).

Different arguments for fairness in trade exist across a broad spectrum of ideologically diverse strategies and practices. The consequence of this is that a term that has as many meanings and applications as this one does, runs the risk of becoming misunderstood at best, and at worst totally meaningless. In particular, it causes confusion for both producers and consumers who must navigate the many articulations of fair trade in the marketplace. Yet how can the ambiguity that results from this cross ownership of fair trade be resolved? A useful start is to begin by working with clear definitions of fair trade. However, it is also important to escape the circular reasoning and largely semantic battle that characterises the current debate over ownership of the fair trade concept, and instead develop ways in which fairness can be measured in the context of specific issues, such as the livelihood of producers in developing countries, which is a key concern of this book.

Is all trade really fair? The theory and practice distinction

Hamilton (2001, p. 62) argues that 'in practice, there is no such thing as free trade'. The theory and practice distinction is a useful one when evaluating an approach and its application. While something may allegedly work in theory, support for that theory will soon wane if it is not effective when applied in practice. Indeed, many have used this distinction to critique and test the legitimacy of the dominant free trade orthodoxy and to illustrate the ineffectiveness of free trade principles in practice, or to point at the absence of these principles in practice. Even so, there is also a danger of using this distinction as a singular defence of an approach: for example, where trade liberalisation advocates defend free trade principles with the call for 'freer trade', citing flaws in current trade practices for market failures. This displays a level of circular reasoning, which is difficult to penetrate. Surely the integrity of free trade principles can be validated by their effectiveness in practice, and as such the responsibility for problems in their application (or lack of application) cannot merely be attributed to the persistence of alternative approaches and practices? In turn, alternative trade principles and practices cannot be supported by citing the failure of free trade alone, but must also be premised on hard evidence establishing their effectiveness. It will certainly be important to move beyond these forms of circular reasoning to enable a consensus on a fair trade strategy in the future. This section evaluates the strength and limitations of the theory and practice distinction by evaluating its application to the debate over free trade.

Defending free trade: Moving beyond semantics

For many advocates of alternative trade practices, the performance of the current trade system under the WTO falls far short of the principles of freedom of exchange. Ramstad (1987, p. 9) claims that the empirical justification for free trade is indeed negligible, and determines 'one cannot help but conclude that it is nothing more than faith in the basic adequacy of the Smithian vision that underlies the economist's advocacy of trade liberalisation'. Despite its role as a multilateral governance institution for trade liberalisation, the WTO struggles to either apply free trade principles holistically or to address the concerns of developing countries.

Mendoza and Bahadur (2002, p. 23) argue that the WTO trade regime, which they characterise as a Global Public Good (GPG), should accordingly provide broad and fair benefit for all its members. Yet, despite the increasing importance of trade for development, they assert that developing countries, in terms of both capacity and resilience, do not participate in or benefit equally from international trade under the current WTO framework (Mendoza and Bahadur, 2002). Walden Bello (in Robinson, 2002) insists that 'in terms of the *practice* of free trade, what it has done really is that it has consolidated the advantages of a number of countries, a minority in the world economy, and this has created structural disadvantages for many of the late comers'.

For Mendoza and Bahadur (2002, p. 19), a key failure in the application of free trade principles under the current WTO system is that it has failed to recognise the relative vulnerability of developing countries which have a diminished capacity to endure 'adjustment costs related to trade liberalisation' and to build a competitive profile beyond low value-added products. Further, the WTO itself structurally disadvantages developing countries, where agreements during the Uruguay Round process produced an 'inherently unequal exchange' between the interests of developed and developing countries (Mendoza and Bahadur, 2002, p. 31). An assessment of the WTO as an exploitative political tool is advanced by Wilkinson (1996, p. 251), who argues that the structural disadvantages facing developing economies deepened with the Uruguay Round process, which saw wealthier industrialised countries 'take advantage of their own economic and technological superiority to further exploit the Third World instead of assisting in its development' (here the impact of Trade Related Property Rights (TRIPS) and Trade Related Investment Measures (TRIMS) is emphasised). In this use of the theory and practice distinction, the authors have highlighted that the WTO primarily provides a tool for political posturing, which severely disadvantages developing countries in trade, promoting an uneven process of trade liberalisation over free trade ideals (see discussion in Chapter 3).

These insights set important challenges for the formulation and practice of the free trade doctrine. Yet, these criticisms are not always taken seriously by free trade advocates who insist that the failures of institutions like the WTO, including a failure to apply free trade principles holistically, can largely be attributed to persisting protectionist forces. A popular defence of failures in free trade practices has been to accuse Fair Trade advocates (who promote alternative trade strategies) of undermining the application of free trade principles through protectionist policies. This concern with protectionist policies is evident in relation to the free trade principle of market access. For Barfield and Irwin (1997) barriers to market access highlight the potential for protectionist policies to undermine the integrity of free trade in practice. They refer to these as one of the many 'pitfalls' that account for the 'constant danger' of 'backsliding on market-opening commitments' developed through multilateral trade negotiations and national unilateral liberalisation (Barfield and Irwin, 1997, p. 26). The concern raised by these authors is that the integrity and full potential of free trade principles and strategies is being undermined by reactionary policies and practices. Thus, the theory and practice distinction is employed to shelter the free trade doctrine by claiming that it is in fact the persistence of protectionist policies, which have undermined the effectiveness of their application. But is it sufficient to defend trade principles and practices in this way?

For Spich (1986) the onus is on free trade advocates to explain why protectionism happens in the first place. He claims that a theory, in this case free trade, 'needs to satisfactorily explain exceptions to the rules as well as confirmation of its basic tenets [and] . . . since protectionism is the most open exception, lecturing against protectionist evils is not sufficient evidence to dismiss it' (Spich, 1986, p. 134). In this sense, Spich conceives of the persistence of protectionist measures, not as a product of reactionary forces trying to undermine free trade, but as a result of the operation of free trade, whether an intended outcome or not. Thus, the challenge is for trade liberalisation advocates to look for answers within their own theories and practices, and not simply to externalise the problems they encounter. Likewise, it is also important that alternative trade advocates do not focus merely on attacking the opposition, but validate their own principles and strategies on the strength of their performance in practice, not least if they seek to establish the legitimacy of alternative trade approaches, despite the call from some free trade critics that alternative trade strategies and practices hide a protectionist agenda.

Fair trade: A guise for protectionism?

In 1938, Freer (1938, p. 303) defined fair trade as the equivalent of 'resale price maintenance', whereby he was referring to a US federal law enacted in 1937. Under this law, manufacturers could seek to set prices by entering into contracts with distributors. In this use of the term, whereby industries are effectively protected, fair trade is often criticised as being simply another label for protectionist policies that insulate domestic firms from the forces of competition under free trade. Essentially, it is understood as a loophole to avoid compliance to the free trade orthodoxy. In fact, Webb (1952, p. 33) characterised it as a 'conspiracy' and a 'wholly deceptive term' which is being used by manufacturers in collusion with retailers to take advantage of consumers by charging higher prices for their products. Equally scathing, Bhagwati (1995, p. 746) claims that 'protectionists see great value in invoking "unfairness" of trade as an argument for getting protection: it is likely to be more successful than simply claiming you cannot hack it and therefore need protection'. In this understanding of fair trade, it is not endowed with the legitimacy or authority of an alternative trade strategy or alternative trade values; rather, it is conceived as an anti-competitive or protectionist strategy to undermine the integrity of free trade for economic gain.

Harmonisation is arguably the dominant conceptualisation of fair trade, which is attacked by trade liberalisation advocates as unfair or protectionist. Harmonisation is identified with strategies such as the social clause, which French (2002, p. 288) depicts as 'the free traders "nightmare" vision . . . presented . . . as little more than a hostile protectionist measure'. Bhagwati and Hudec (1996a, 1996b) published a two-volume (economic and legal) analysis on *Fair Trade and Harmonization*. Both volumes generally reassert the benefits of trade liberalisation in international trade, illustrating the uptake in the trade liberalisation literature on the task of defining and critiquing Fair Trade and its strategies. In fact, the legitimacy of Fair Trade from this perspective is only premised upon the question whether Fair Trade is a necessary 'prerequisite for free trade' for the purpose of achieving a 'level playing field' (Bhagwati, 1996, p. 1). Moreover, Fair Trade is considered synonymous with demands for the harmonisation of environmental and labour standards. Bhagwati (1996, p. 5) argues that such demands largely reflect concern in developed economies that competition with 'low-standard' economies will manifest the reduction or loss of higher standards in developed economies. He maintains that these demands could also be viewed by developing economies as protectionist measures, whereby 'high standard countries may deliberately set their standards selectively and at high levels to impose excessive costs on their rivals in the low-standard countries' (Bhagwati, 1996, p. 5). Thus, Fair Trade is not even considered an ultimate challenge to the authority of free trade, merely as a possible prerequisite. The argument that it may serve as a necessary forerunner to free trade is also, ultimately, rejected.

Bhagwati also attacks the legitimacy of demands for Fair Trade and harmonisation from a different perspective. He asserts that the demands made by developed economies in this regard, may simply reflect 'transborder moral concerns' and, accordingly, the legitimacy of such demands rests on testing 'the moral soundness of these standards' (Bhagwati, 1996, pp. 1–2). In this analysis, Fair Trade is conceived as a concept laden with moral values and he argues that if standards are understood as 'culture specific', where what is morally right in one country 'may actually be morally wicked' in another, then harmonisation policies can be seen as an attempt to impose moral values on countries in which they have no natural authority. Essentially, Bhagwati interprets Fair Trade as the projection of both an economic and a moral power struggle between developed and developing economies, between rich and poor countries, whereby wealthier countries are both attempting to protect their economies and to impose their moral values globally. Thus Fair Trade would ultimately have the effect of disadvantaging poorer countries 'if the standards are legitimately different, for example, in the poor countries, and if they are "harmonised up" by force of sanctions, including trade sanctions, by the rich countries, that will ipso facto harm the poor countries' (Bhagwati, 1996, p. 5). In this sense, Fair Trade, specifically the argument for Fair Trade as a prerequisite for free trade, is conceived as anything but fair.

While accusations of protectionist policies and practices serve as a commonplace defence of failures in free trade practices, the question this poses for alternative trade practices is twofold. First, does the label of protectionism fit? Second, even if it does fit, is protectionism itself such a bad thing? Some scholars adamantly reject the protectionist label preferring to don the Fair Trade label instead, while others maintain that being accused of having a protectionist agenda is not so unfair after all, claiming that protection is indeed a necessary element of fairness in trade.

Hamilton (2001) makes a distinct departure from Bhagwati's view that Fair Trade and harmonisation is more likely to facilitate a protectionist or transborder moral agenda. He draws attention to the fact that WTO rules already constrain some forms of trade based on moral standards using the example of discrimination against products produced using prison labour (Hamilton, 2001, p. 62). He explains that Fair Trade-advocating standards can be developed through international consultation and administered through the WTO framework for trade. Hamilton (2001, p. 64) thereby rejects that this form of standard setting can be branded as protectionist. While Bhagwati limits his analysis to unilateral enforcement of standards, thereby branding harmonisation as protectionist, Hamilton is able to avoid this label by considering different strategies for developing and administering standards in trade, including strategies already in place in the WTO trade framework.

John (2001) takes a different approach to this issue by making a distinction between the call for rights and the call for standards. He considers the issue of Fair Trade from the perspective of developing countries, specifically, 'commodity-producing countries' (John, 2001, pp. 64, 67). He uses the example of the Indian Campaign for labour rights to examine the issue and identifies two separate strategies for labour rights, distinguished by emphasis on either standards (exogenously determined) or rights (endogenously determined) (John, 2001, p. 67). He insists that exogenously set standards potentially shift the responsibility and execution of standards from labour in the developing countries to corporations, employers and consumers, and that non-compliance to standards determined in developed countries also tends to involve trade sanctions (John, 2001, pp. 67–9). Alternatively, rights denote a more 'organic' process, and develop as a part of the growing 'self-awareness and organisation' of labour itself (John, 2001, p. 67). Essentially, John argues that rights are a more sustainable and empowering strategy for achieving improved conditions and standards. A standards approach runs the risk of undermining the sovereignty of developing countries that are forced to abide by them. This argument shows an uptake on the type of criticism that was made by Bhagwati and ultimately sets a challenge to Bhagwati's conceptualisation of Fair Trade as protectionism.

The so-called protectionist interpretation of Fair Trade raises an important issue in the debate over free trade. Should domestic industries and especially their labour markets be protected from free trade, either wholly or during a process of adjustment? Ramstad (1987) argues that this is necessary, and advocates protectionist or otherwise Fair Trade policies by this authority. He relies on John Commons' 'Theory of Reasonable Value' (Ramstad, 1987) to attack the logic of free trade policies, arguing that collectively generated rules, as manifest in the US legal system, *are* central to the operation of the current trade system, and that '"fairness" appears to be [and indeed, should be] the real criterion by which the acceptability of trade practices is judged' (Ramstad, 1987, p. 22). In particular, Ramstad expresses his concern with the effect globalisation is having on workers' wages in the US, arguing that there is a justification for protectionist or Fair Trade policies that mitigate this negative effect on workers' standards of living. In this context, Fair Trade, a concept developed to help developing countries' producers, is conceived as a necessary remedy to the detrimental effect that free trade is having on the industries and labour markets of developed economies.

In some respects, accusations of protectionism have forced alternative trade advocates to take a critical look at their principles and practices. Some of the insights they have gained have been discussed in this chapter. However, as fair trade is subject to reinterpretation according to distinct and often opposed value sets, this debate over labels has often devolved into an ideological stand-off, which cannot be resolved. Spich (1986, pp. 139, 141) explains that while trade liberalisation emphasises the combined values of 'freedom, efficiency and competition', policy conflict arises when these dominant values are 'pitted against values of equity and fairness' (identified as values intrinsic to Fair Trade). Here, Fair Trade is defined in opposition to free trade according to an alternative value set and, accordingly, the dialogue between free and Fair Trade is perceived to revolve around a debate over values. This is distinct from Bhagwati's (1996) assertion of moral values under Fair Trade policies serving either a protectionist agenda, or being culturally bound and thereby inappropriate as universal standards. Fair Trade in this context asserts that free trade itself operates according to a distinct set of values, essentially economic ones, and that trade should seek social outcomes through the implementation of social values as well. In fact, Raynolds (2000) claims that this conception of Fair Trade is setting a clear and deliberate challenge to the authority of the free trade system and its ideology. She asserts that Fair Trade initiatives effectively challenge the logic of basing competition in the market place on the price mechanism alone, by striving 'to make transparent the relations under which commodities are exchanged', a process she refers to as 'social re-embedding' (Raynolds, 2000, p. 298).

Kinnock (1994, p. 124) also asserts a moral rationale for reforming the conduct of international trade, insisting that 'there has to be an ethical basis for economic endeavour'. This is echoed by Maseland and de Vaal (2002) who emphasise the moral premise of a Fair Trade argument for development through trade. By fusing development priorities with trade, they argue that Fair Trade rests on the assumption that there is a moral obligation to ensure that producers receive fair prices and operate 'under decent conditions' (Maseland and de Vaal, 2002, p. 251). This moral imperative is based on 'an idea that justice lies underneath the Fair Trade concept', where Fair Trade in practice is in fact 'an operationalisation of an idea of what just trade would be' (Maseland and de Vaal, 2002, p. 252). They assert that this conception of Fair Trade has emerged from 'the consumer movement' in many Western countries, with consumers increasingly participating in 'pro-poor trade with developing countries' (Maseland and de Vaal, 2002, p. 252). They insist, however, that this form of Fair Trade is clearly distinct from 'fair trade that calls for protectionist measures', where developed countries are trying to protect their own industries from cheap imports from developing countries (Maseland and de Vaal, 2002, p. 252). Rather, the argument is put forward that trade must be based on a notion of justice, whereby development priorities are emphasised in trade.

Whether there is a 'war of words' or irreconcilable differences in core values to overcome, it is clear that an understanding of best practice to achieve 'fair trade' will not be resolved through abstract arguments. Rather, 'the proof is in the pudding' as they say – or if you will – any articulation of fair trade should rise and fall on an evaluation of its merits in practice.

Conclusion

Understanding fair trade arguments and strategies is near impossible when armed with an expectation of a single definition or body of work. A 'Fair Trade Manifesto', which sets out a distinct theoretical framework that economists can debate in their journals and classrooms, simply does not exist. A more realistic expectation is to anticipate a live debate, in which participants deliberate and argue over the legitimacy and achievements of free trade principles and practices. A debate within which understandings of fairness in trade are passionately proffered and, no doubt, vehemently contested. Similar to the teachers, parents and students who may hold different points of view on what is fair in the playground largely based on differences in their experiences and priorities, Fair Traders are a diverse group typically divided by differences in ideology and agenda. How do we traverse this ideologically divided terrain? An important point of entry into identifying and understanding the different approaches to fair trade is to delineate the different voices and arguments for what is fair in trade. It then becomes possible to see that the fair trade debate – valuable in itself as an arena of contestation on trading principles and practices – has also produced a range of coherent approaches, and often rigorous models for redefining international trade.

In this chapter five key arguments for fairness in trade have been identified: differentiating between a freedom, rights linkage, value distribution, ecological sustainability and business accountability approach. This conceptual framework provides a clear distinction between a trade liberalisation argument for fair trade, which supports current trade practices, and alternative models that typically seek some level of reform or replacement in current trade practices. While advocates of alternative trade strategies and practices (which identify as Fair Trade) reject free trade by attacking the legitimacy of principles of freedom and current trade practices, it is important to test whether alternative trade models perform any better in facilitating development goals. Essentially, to pose the question: do alternative trade principles and practices support sustainable development? The underlying claim in this endeavour is that Fair Trade advocates should justify and legitimate alternative approaches to trade, not only upon the failures of a free trade orthodoxy but also by similarly testing and then refining their own principles and practices. This would allow Fair Trade, as an alternative approach, to grow in strength by ensuring that it is able to define and improve principles and methods, which are empirically justified. Use of the label 'fair' should not only be debated through multiple interpretations of the word but also through empirical research that evaluates different Fair Trade arguments by identifying and testing the principles they advocate. The following chapters aim to contribute to this endeavour.

3
The Market: An Unequal Exchange?

The claim is put forward that the terms of international trade disadvantage developing countries and are inherently unfair or unequal. This has placed trade at the centre of development debates with calls from many NGOs that 'trade not aid' should be the focus of development policies. Rather than questioning a link between trade and development per se, questions have been raised over the elevation of the market as the key institutional form for regulating trade. Critics also claim the market is neither free nor fair in its current institutional articulation, with uneven deregulation favouring developed countries over the developing countries that have lowered their trade barriers more rapidly. In the debate over trade and development, the role and limitations of the market – both as an ideal but also particularly at the level of implementation – remain divisive. For some a return to a more regulated trade environment – or at the very least a move to a more evenly deregulated trade environment – is crucial before trade can begin to serve the needs of developing countries.

An evaluation of these arguments requires an examination of the operation of the free market on multiple levels: as an idea (in theory), at the level of implementation (examining associated policies and manifest institutional frameworks) and in practice (measuring performance in markets). The structure of economies over time, and understandings of pathways for development, has – to a great extent – mirrored the logic of prevailing economic theories. Economic policies and practices are sometimes justified on the abstract merits of the bodies of high theory from which they draw their legitimacy, even when they fail to perform in the real world. As such the first section of this chapter will examine free trade as an idea and some of the contestation over its capacity to promote development, before turning to an evaluation of the implementation and the performance of associated practices in subsequent sections.

Broadly, this chapter problematises the operation of the free market from the point of view of developing countries. This includes examination of the global governance of trade, historically and through the WTO in particular, to identify the relative voice and influence of developing and developed countries. Analysis focuses on agricultural trade as developing countries typically specialise in the production and exchange of agricultural products. With consideration of the conditions of trade for a range of agricultural commodities – particularly focusing on coffee – it becomes clear that trade through conventional pathways remains an inherently unequal exchange. Persistent inequity in trade under the WTO regime suggests further reflection on the logic and implementation of free market policies is needed.

Contesting the logic of the free market

The principle of freedom of exchange was developed long before it began to dominate international policy debates and even before the process of trade liberalisation began in the wake of World War II. The principle draws its theoretic legitimacy from the important works of classical economists, Adam Smith and David Ricardo, as well as others who further developed and refined what has grown into the body of contemporary economic theory taught in classrooms today called 'neoclassical economics'. Smith [1789] (in Cannan, 1904, IV.3.32) proposed that international trade would be 'mutually beneficial' for countries that participate. He argued that specialisation in production and trade would manifest greater efficiency domestically and globally, further serving the interests of the populace of every country by ensuring that they could now 'buy whatever they want of those who sell it cheapest' (Smith [1789], in Cannan 1904, IV.3.39). Smith argued that countries should export that which they had an absolute advantage to produce and trade (i.e. they could do so more cheaply than any other country), and that they should import those products which they had a disadvantage in (i.e. they could not produce and trade as cheaply as another). Ricardo (1821) refined Smith's argument regarding specialisation by claiming that countries would also benefit from producing and trading goods in which they had a 'comparative advantage'. Using a now famous two-country (Portugal and England), two-product (cloth and wine) illustration, he explained that while Portugal could enjoy an absolute advantage in both cloth and wine production, it would be better positioned to focus production in wine in which it had the most favourable advantage. Portugal had more to gain in expanding wine production, which would overcompensate losses from importing cloth, thus England would gain a comparative advantage in cloth production and trade.

Before the promise of mutual gains from international trade, there was no real incentive to expand the horizons of the domestic economy beyond its geographical borders, except for products a country could not produce itself. The principle of comparative advantage was also used as vehicle to explain how specialisation in production and exchange would better serve a domestic economy. Indeed together, these principles laid the groundwork for propelling understanding of a country's food security away from the principle of self-sufficiency to one of reliance on incomes and thereby food imports from global markets. What is most important about these theoretical assertions is the general proposition that open trade is compatible with, and will advance a country's economic interests, including food security. This assumes that countries are on a relatively level playing field in terms of their capacities and areas of specialisation, despite the fact that most of the so-called developed countries relied on domestic industry, especially manufacturing, and have historically used protectionist policies liberally, including for food production. Yet free trade, in theory, suggests that countries can benefit from, and develop on the back of, their export industries.

These works and others laid the foundation for an emerging development specialisation in the field of economics, with 'development economics' emerging as a separate branch within this discipline after World War II (Szentes, 2005, p. 146). A leading pioneer of this new branch of economics was Arthur Lewis (in Esteva, 1992, p. 12), who in the 1950s argued that development as a concept was fundamentally tied to aspirations of 'economic growth'. This approach gained momentum and was rearticulated through the rising authority of neoclassical economics, which picked up on the classical ideas espoused by Smith and Ricardo, emphasising the free market as the key engine for growth and development. Thus an export-oriented growth formula became the mantra of economic development scholars, as well as the emerging neoliberal policy framework, which won favour in the 1980s. Dubbed the 'Washington Consensus', this new development approach focused on market enabling policies such as privatisation and deregulation (Williamson, 1990). The vision of development became tied to self-regulating markets, with government responsibility for development curtailed to that of a facilitator, simply enabling the free operation of the market and the benefits this was heralded to bring to society at large.

This formula for development, however, is highly contested. For example, dependency theorists see international trade as an engine for exploitation rather than growth-led development. Pioneers such as André Gunder Frank (1966) argued that 'first world' economies were harnessing trade for their own development, at the expense of 'third world' economies. Vandana Shiva (1989), critical of the commodification of development and its impact on women and the environment, advanced an ecological feminist critique of conventional development theories. In a similar vein, Amartya Sen (see 1989, 1999) also critical of the commodification of development rejected the orthodox conflation of development with 'economic development'. He viewed '[d]evelopment . . . as a process of expanding the real freedoms that people enjoy' (Sen, 1999, p. 3). Such freedoms include economic freedoms, but also social and political freedoms. Apparent in these varied critiques of orthodox theories of development is a concern with the projected benefits of a market-oriented approach to development – and indeed – with the economic reductionism with which development as a project is typically approached. Essentially, faith in the market as the central driver for development is placed under a microscope. A discord over the primacy of the market in development is clearly evident at the level of theorising; however, it is also evident at the level of implementation of market enabling policies. On closer examination, efforts to implement trade liberalisation have a chequered history at best, with clear limits on the commitment to free markets evident in the historic treatment of agriculture in particular.

Implementing free market policies: Cross-institutional regulatory pressures

Paradoxically, a process of deregulation depends on exactly that which it aims to do away with: regulatory measures. Working under the ethos of market liberalisation, many countries (though certainly not all) have forfeited significant regulatory powers. However, these powers have actually been transferred into global and regional regulatory apparatuses and institutions. The significance of this is that there are political processes behind governance in a free trade regime that contradict the idealised vision of 'unfettered' market forces. In examining the evolution of global regulatory capacity geared towards trade liberalisation, it becomes clear that historically two distinct institutional umbrellas emerged and became politically contested. The contest over institutional pathways was very political in nature and irrevocably impacted on both the voice of developing countries, and also the status that agriculture would ultimately gain in the trade liberalisation process.

Three pillars of the multilateral trade regime

The vision and push for trade liberalisation was launched at the end of World War II, which marked a shift from old to new world powers, providing the victors of the war – particularly the US and Great Britain – an opportunity to take a leading role in the design and implementation of a new model for the global economy. Indeed, the WTO multilateral trade regime was described by the United States Trade Representative (USTR, 2000) as reflecting 'more than fifty years of U.S. leadership in creating an open, international, rules based trading system that yields real benefits for American workers, farmers, businesses, and consumers'. The blueprint for post-war reconstruction and a new global architecture was the Bretton Woods Agreement of 1944. This agreement outlined plans for three institutional arms for the post-war economy: the IMF, the International Board for Reconstruction and Development (later renamed the World Bank), and the International Trade Organisation (ITO). However, the third envisioned 'pillar' – the ITO, was not created (Howse and Trebilcock, 2002, pp. 20–1), thereby leaving a significant breach in the institutional capacity and integrity of the Bretton Woods trade liberalisation model (by not instituting the envisioned balance of power). It also created the possibility for trade liberalisation to take two distinct pathways. Indeed, the current multilateral trade regime – particularly regarding its treatment of agriculture – evolved over two important phases. During an interim phase, while the formation of the ITO was still debated, agriculture remained protected, while half a century later, the formation of the WTO instead of the envisioned ITO, heralded in a new permanent phase and with it trade liberalisation in agriculture.

The creation of the ITO would have entailed adoption of the Havana Charter, which set out a special role and special rules for agricultural production and trade, emphasising a goal to stabilise agricultural commodity production and trade through supply management. The Havana Charter for an ITO (UNCTE, 1948), albeit never ratified by the 53 countries that were signatories to the Charter (Kravis, 1968, p. 304), established fundamental principles that would guide the structure and operation of International Commodity Agreements across a range of primary commodities. The Charter recognised that primary commodities may require special treatment in trade, through intergovernmental agreements which would, when necessary, endorse and implement some form of regulation. The Havana Charter recognised that, left to market forces alone, primary commodities were particularly vulnerable to market failure. It argued that 'the conditions under which some primary commodities are produced, exchanged and consumed are such that international trade in these commodities may be affected by special difficulties', including a tendency towards 'disequilibrium between production ad consumption', 'accumulation of burdensome stocks' and 'fluctuations in prices' (UNCTE, 1948, Article 55, p. 51). The argument that primary commodities are beset by unique difficulties, which cannot be remedied as a function of supply and demand in a free market, raises an important critique of the capacity of market forces to adequately service the trade of agricultural commodities.

While International Commodity Agreements were established to address these concerns, they had no real legitimacy without the adoption of the Charter and creation of the ITO. To fill the gap, a provisional agreement was negotiated, the General Agreement on Tariffs and Trade (GATT) 1947, which was intended to serve as a forerunner to the creation of the ITO (Howse and Trebilcock, 2002, p. 21), yet made no real provisions for agriculture. As such, the future of the ITO became an important point of contention between developed and developing countries, primarily over the issue of relative representation and voice in the multilateral trade regime and the status of agriculture. Twin pathways for the multi-lateral trade regime became apparent: the ITO pathway as championed by developing countries, especially in the forum of the United Nations Conference on Trade and Development (UNCTAD), and GATT pathway (later GATT/WTO), which garnered more support from the developed countries. The call for UNCTAD in 1964 itself was a result of a push from developing countries to create an alternative international forum on trade issues (Howse and Trebilcock, 2002, p. 22). The importance of agricultural commodity trade on UNCTAD agenda underlined the inability of GATT to prioritise and cater to one of the fundamental concerns of developing countries. Accordingly, 'a great deal of international trade negotiations took place within UNCTAD (and not GATT), and the major issues related to commodities' (Khor, 2005, p. 10). Indeed, it was at UNCTADs quadren-nial conferences, and not at GATT, that the revival of the ITO concept was discussed (Raghavan, 1997, p. 3). UNCTAD stood as a testament to the exclusion that developing countries felt under GATT regime, and the hopes they voiced for a more inclusive alternative to GATT regime. The eventual formation of the WTO in 1994 cemented the death of the ITO, and led to a final and formal departure from commodity stabilisation schemes as envisioned in the Havana Charter and facilitated in the absence of the creation of the ITO by UNCTAD (see discussion in chapter 3).

The Uruguay Round of international trade negotiations (1986–94) laid the groundwork for the eventual formation in 1994 of the WTO and a new permanent phase for the multilateral trade architecture. The WTO applied GATT 1947, for those that were signatories to it, as well as GATT 1994 and other agreements for *all* WTO members. The WTO approach is described as a 'single undertaking approach . . . [where] membership in the WTO entails accepting all the results of the Round without exception' (WTO, 2006). The significance of this is that the depth and breadth of trade liberalisation is now extended through membership in the new WTO regime, and areas such as agriculture are now also subject to trade liberalisation reform for all members. While GATT 1947 had applied to agriculture as well, 'it contained loopholes' such as sanctioning the ongoing use of non-tariff measures including import quotas and subsidies (WTO, 2012). The Uruguay Round brought agriculture firmly on board through the adoption of the Agreement on Agriculture (AoA), although negotiations on agriculture have continued since the AoA came into force in 2000.

Before looking at the impact of the AoA on agriculture in this second permanent phase, the scope of trade liberalisation in agriculture during the interim phase is worthy of consideration. While agriculture was a hot potato on GATT agenda, the World Bank and IMF did not have any qualms in advancing trade liberalisation in developing countries through their own activities. These two pillars of the global multilateral trading regime have a unique governance structure based on a 'one dollar – one vote' schema (Raghavan, 1997, p. 24), giving wealthy countries most of the decision-making power. There can be no argument that the governance structure of both these institutions is therefore skewed in favour of the wealthy economies. Indeed, the World Bank and IMF have served as ideal institutions through which developed countries demanded deeper trade liberalisation measures from developing countries than they were willing to undertake themselves. Primarily under the loan conditionalities imposed by the World Bank and IMF, more so even than under the AoA today, developing country farmers were 'exposed to excessive and rapid import liberalisation' (Khor, 2005, p. 8). Any possibility of escaping this fate was largely undermined by the impact of the 1982 debt crisis, which 'hugely increased the power and influence of the World Bank and the IMF over low-income countries' (Buckman, 2005, p. 229). Indeed, Buckman (2005, p. 229) estimates that the World Bank and IMF have managed approximately 40 per cent of the world's economies since the debt crisis began.

The World Bank and IMF played an important role in undermining the price stabilisation schemes that the interim GATT system had tolerated thus far. IMF and World Bank conditionalities saw the disbandment of state-run marketing boards (Buckman, 2005, p. 229), which had previously assisted the development of agricultural commodity industries like coffee. The policies of these institutions contributed to a disjunction in the pace and intensity of trade liberalisation between developed and developing economies (see discussion further on) and greatly impacted on commodity stabilisation schemes. More importantly, the World Bank and IMF interpretation of regulatory measures facilitating trade liberalisation was and remains strongly paternalistic, usurping the traditional role of governments themselves in managing their own economies. Thus, while the two institutions used regulation to further trade liberalisation, they did so employing interventionist regulatory measures akin to those employed in the government-managed economies that the process of trade liberalisation aims to ameliorate. This quasi-paternalistic mode of regulation, albeit in the name of trade liberalisation, continues to this day, and ensures that the process of trade liberalisation is applied differently in developing and developed economies through the lack of continuity and conformity in the respective approaches of the three pillars of the international trade regime.

The treatment of developing countries in agriculture

For the longest time, the World Bank, WTO and IMF have not synchronised their policies and essentially have gone so far as to create different rules for different countries and on different issues. The WTO's AoA at the Uruguay Round in 1994 is a prime example of this. The AoA stipulates member commitments and criteria with the vision of upholding an overarching objective 'to establish a fair and market-oriented agricultural trading system' (WTO, 1994). This objective is defined as entailing reductions of protections and supports. While developing and least developed countries (LDCs) have been provided differential status in terms of reduced reduction targets and additional time to meet these targets, in one important area of 'green box' supports, which remain sanctioned under the AoA, developing countries and LDCs have already 'achieved' large reductions, if not complete loss of supports and protections through earlier and ongoing World Bank and IMF loan conditionalities. While the World Bank and IMF continue to mandate reduction of green box protections through loan conditionalities, the AoA does not factor in the reality of the 'extra' commitments and conditionality imposed on a large number of developing countries relative to their developed country counterparts.

Khor (2005, p. 9) argues that the AoA is 'imbalanced in favour of . . . developed countries' who, through the capacity to afford high subsidies, largely avoid the trade liberalisation pressures they work to impose on developing countries. The AoA effectively sanctions agricultural support mechanisms that favour one group of countries over another. Subsidies sanctioned under the AoA are typical for industrialised countries, and their use ensures that large agribusiness enterprises, from countries like the US and within the EU, veritably engage in 'massive dumping of under-priced agrifood products in developing countries' (International Union of Food, Agriculture, Hotel, Restaurant, Catering, Tobacco and Allied Workers' Association, 2002, p. 10). The World Bank (2007, p. 97) notes that while support for agricultural producers in member countries of the Organisation for Economic Co-operation and Development (OECD) fell as a percentage of total farm receipts between 1986 and 2005,[1] it increased from $242 billion to $273 billion a year. Essentially, the implementation of free trade in agriculture, through the regulatory apparatus of the AoA by the WTO, maintains an uneven imposition of trade liberalisation burdens on developed and developing economies and gives developed countries an unfair advantage over developing countries and LDCs. This is reflected in tensions over market access.

Market access, and in particular access to value added markets, remains a prominent issue for developing countries. A common argument is that the 'rules that govern it [world trade] are rigged in favour of the rich' (Oxfam, 2002, p. 5). Even free trade advocates are quick to point out the failure of the WTO regime to provide an equitable market access outcome across the board. Jagdish Bhagwati (in Robinson, 2002) is critical of the high tariffs and subsidies maintained by the wealthier OECD countries, particularly in the area of agriculture, claiming that in the case of the US 'we have actually used the WTO consistent procedures to increase protection'. What impact have highly protectionist policies had on the developing nations, which rely on volatile commodities such as coffee for their foreign exchange earnings? Kevin Cleaver, former Director of the Agriculture and Rural Development Department of the World Bank, claimed that barriers to trade 'represent a limit to the options for diversification to other crops and value added processes' (World Bank, 2003). Oxfam (2002, p. 5) insists that the loss in potential revenue, both through diversification and value-added processing, could be as much as $100 billion annually, 'twice as much as they receive in aid'. Thus, while developing nations are forced 'to open their markets at breakneck speed' under the conditions imposed by IMF and World Bank structural adjustment programmes (SAPs), the retention of highly protectionist policies in the wealthier nations has locked the poorer nations of the world into 'low value-added ghettoes' (Oxfam, 2002, p. 6). Essentially, the barriers to new and value-added markets have created an unhealthy dependency on a range of commodities.

It is not surprising that in the 2002 trade talks, developing countries were concerned to revisit the issue of agricultural protections. The Doha round, which was presented by developed countries and the [WTO] Secretariat as a 'development round', (Third World Network, 2002) should surely have prioritised some of the key inequities in agricultural trade liberalisation on its agenda. A Joint Statement of NGOs and Social Movements (Third World Network, 2002) instead claimed that the trade round was more appropriately described as 'everything but development' or 'a development disaster'. A key reason for this was that the Doha Declaration sought to introduce a new range of issues, 'investment, competition, transparency in government procurement ... [and] trade facilitation', an agenda, which was generally opposed by developing countries (Third World Network, 2002; see also Bello, 2005, p. 158). Polaski (2007, p. 1) argues that the talks have indeed 'stalemated over agricultural trade'. A key issue for the stalemate is the proposal that developing countries should further open their agricultural markets (Polaski, 2007, pp. 2–4), while one of the key arguments made by developing countries[2] is that they should be able to maintain some level of tariff protection for vital agricultural products (which are fundamental to concerns such as food security) (Polaski, 2007, p. 4). The Doha round highlights that the relative mechanisms afforded developing countries for the protection of their agricultural industries is still a key issue which fails to be addressed in the multilateral trade regime.

The tensions between regionalism and multilateralism

While the story of the process of trade liberalisation through global institutional regulatory measures is complicated, there is yet another important element to the dispersed and contradictory character of governance under the conditions of the global trade liberalisation framework. The analysis earlier in this chapter identified a contest between twin pathways in the early stages of the Bretton Woods system. Dunkley (2000) identifies a new twin pathways dilemma that again places the process of trade liberalisation at a crossroad. He explains that 'two partly competing modes of transport are currently in use – regionalism and multilateralism' (Dunkley, 2000, p. 4). While the Havana model and the WTO model envisioned and applied a very different treatment of agriculture, Stoeckel (1998, p. 19) notes that 'preferential regional trading arrangements' are criticised for undermining the principles of 'equal treatment' that underpins GATT. Stoeckel and Borrel (2001, p. ix) take this criticism on board, arguing that preferential trade through devices such as regional trade agreements 'send[s] the wrong message – that discriminatory trade is acceptable'. Yet not all forms of regionalism are necessarily perceived to undermine the integrity of multilateral trading arrangements.

Stoeckel (1998, p. 19) puts forward that 'open regionalism', with the example of the Asia-Pacific Economic Cooperation (APEC), provides 'another avenue' of non-discriminatory regionalism, which does not undermine the multilateral trade regime. Ravenhill (1999, p. 266) explains that APEC is 'unique among regional economic groupings' because of its commitment to open regionalism, whereby 'trade concessions that APEC economies made would be extended on a non-discriminatory basis to other members of the WTO.' However, the example of regionalism clearly demonstrates that the trading regime is not merely centrally regulated through the auspices of the WTO, but rather, whether under conditions of open or closed regionalism, regional institutions (both the regional agreements and the regional associations that develop them) create additional levels of regulation within the international trade regime. This can also be observed with the example of regional development banks (i.e. the regional counterparts to the IMF and World Bank), such as the Asian Development Bank (ADB), and can further be observed on a unilateral level through individual trade agreements negotiated between countries. Yet despite these multifarious and uneven sources of regulation, developing countries remain strongly tied to participating in global markets. The characteristics of dependency on agricultural production and trade, in particular, help us to gain a deeper understanding of the dynamics of the international trade regime.

Developing countries, agriculture and engagement in global markets

Robbins (2003, p. 6) notes that '[d]eveloping countries have a group of resources – in the form of agricultural products, which can only be produced in tropical regions – that the developed world cannot, or will not, do without'. This, according to Robbins (2003, p. 6), should provide developing countries with a very strong 'card' to play 'in the game of international commerce'. Developing countries might appear to have a natural advantage in agricultural production and trade for some agricultural goods, but the capacity to play this card effectively is, as Robbins' own work recognises, currently very limited. Developing countries' engagement in global markets must be understood with reference to the particular opportunities and constraints that developing countries face, and which will interact – positively or negatively – with the rules of international trade outlined in the previous section. Agricultural commodities, as the Havana Charter affirmed more than half a century ago, are highly volatile at both the level of production (i.e. the high variations in supply) and (connected to this) how they trade (i.e. the prices they command). High national debt burdens and generally poor socio-economic conditions (including poor producers that remain painfully dependent on these commodities with limited ability to respond to poor market conditions), feed into this dependency. Thus, with reference to the high reliance on agriculture given the poor performance of agricultural commodities in global markets, and also considering the socio-economic context of production, it becomes difficult to even suggest that the free market can offer a level playing field for developed and developing economies alike. While the free market thesis assumes the ability of producers to respond to market signals, this assumption falls flat when we examine the position of developing countries in global markets.

In its specialised report on agriculture – *World Development Report 2008: Agriculture for Development* – the World Bank (2007, p. 3) estimated that close to half of the population in developing countries live in rural areas with approximately 86 per cent deriving a livelihood from agriculture. Drawing on 2002 figures, it further estimated that 'three [out] of every four poor people in developing countries live in rural areas' (World Bank, 2007, p. 1). Differentiating between 'agriculture-based' (predominantly Sub-Saharan Africa), 'transforming' (comprising countries in South and East Asia as well as the Middle East and North Africa) and 'urbanised' (including Latin American, European and Central Asian) countries, the World Bank noted that agriculture represented 29 per cent, 13 per cent and 6 per cent of gross domestic product (GDP) in 2005 respectively (World Bank, 2007, pp. 1–5). However, the importance of agriculture is better understood through its share of the labour force, especially for developing countries. For example, approximately 65 per cent of the labour force in agriculture-based economies is working in agriculture (World Bank, 2007, p. 3). Typically reliance on agriculture, as measured by share of GDP and labour force, is higher in the poorest countries, and a gap can be observed between figures relating to agriculture's share of GDP and those relating to its share of the labour force (World Bank, 2007, p. 27). This gap is explained in part by the relative use of labour by different industries (e.g. agriculture is often more labour intensive than other sectors, like extractive industries). It is also explained by differences in the relative importance of formal agricultural markets to rural livelihoods. The World Bank (2007, p. 75) explains that rural households rely on a range of livelihood strategies, including, for example, incomes from markets, production for subsistence living and incomes from farm or non-farm wage labour. For example, in Nigeria 60 per cent of rural households were classified as 'subsistence oriented' and over 11 per cent as 'market-oriented' in 2004 (World Bank, 2007, p. 76). As livelihoods derived from subsistence living do not appear on the ledgers for national accounts, the GDP share of agriculture often under-represents the importance of agriculture to an economy.

What these figures do show is that poor people in poor countries are heavily reliant on building a livelihood based on agriculture. In terms of engagement in global markets, there is an existing capacity as well as untapped potential to produce for global agricultural markets. For agriculture-based economies, most of which derive a large share of their foreign exchange earnings from agriculture (World Bank, 2007, p. 34), it is an imperative to maximise incomes from the agricultural commodities in which they specialise. Typically developing countries export traditional agricultural commodities from the non-staple crop sector, although diversification into alternatives like vegetables, flowers and fish is increasing (World Bank, 2007, p. 32). Developing countries might need to assess the sustainability of livelihoods based on selling traditional non-food agricultural commodities into global markets versus developing and improving domestic markets and subsistence livelihoods. While prices have rallied in recent years, longitudinal data for a range of these commodities, including, for example, cocoa, cotton, sugar and tea (see World Bank 2012a, 2012b, 2012c, 2012d; see also discussion of coffee in the following section), illustrate high volatility, including periodic price hikes but also protracted periods of price decline and even crisis. While price volatility is a predictable outcome in the trade of agricultural goods, often due to unforeseen circumstances such as weather conditions, price averages are generally lower since the advent of trade liberalisation in agriculture.

Considering the poor performance of agricultural commodities over time for developing countries, it would appear that alternative sources of income would be more beneficial. Nevertheless developing countries and poor people within them remain tied to the production of these crops for a number of reasons. In the first instance, it is important to remember that historically, both the IMF and the World Bank promoted cash crop production as part of their advocacy of an export-led growth model for developing countries. For example, Slob (2006, p. 124) notes that in many cases countries were advised to grow coffee for export income by the IMF and World Bank, including a massive promotion of coffee by the World Bank in Vietnam. These traditional agricultural commodities, which are traded on the international market, bring in vital dollars, which fuel the engine of developing countries' economies. It is this ability to bring in cash which has earned such commodities the nickname 'cash crops'. For a number of LDCs, which are highly reliant on cash crops for foreign exchange earnings (ICO, 2005) non-staple food exports like coffee are considered especially important. Across 2005–10, coffee accounted for more than 10 per cent of the value of total exports for eight countries, including 70 per cent for Timor-Leste and 28 per cent for Rwanda (International Trade Centre, 2012, p. 2). Additionally, developing countries, and agricultural producers within them, operate in often very challenging conditions with low socioeconomic indicators and poor infrastructure serving as severe constraints to prospects of diversification and value-added processing. Essentially, growers lack the skills to move into alternative income-generating ventures (Robbins, 2003, p. 17). Indeed, these kinds of constraints, where producers 'must continue to produce . . . no matter how low the market price falls', have led Robbins (2003, p. 17) to conclude that '[t]he markets for these primary products . . . do not behave in the same way as markets for most manufactured goods'. As such, the performance of global commodity markets such as coffee, considered next, need to be examined with bearing these constraints in mind.

The coffee market

Aside from serving as a flagship product for Fairtrade, coffee allows a case study for the integration of developing countries into global markets. Coffee is a crop that can only be produced in tropical climates, and by default is predominantly produced in developing countries. It is also a product that is primarily consumed in developed countries (Daviron and Ponte, 2005, p. 50) and thus can highlight the dynamics of the sometimes divergent interests of developed and developing countries in trade. In the case of coffee, we also see the most vulnerable producers exposed to the vagaries of the global market with the estimate that approximately 70 per cent of global coffee is produced by smallholder producers, on small plots under five hectares (Fitter and Kaplinsky, 2001, p. 14). An evaluation of the impact of trade liberalisation on the coffee market highlights some of the challenges that developing countries and their coffee producers face in engaging the global market, as well as the worsening conditions they have experienced through the trade liberalisation of this important agricultural commodity.

Trade liberalisation and transition from supply management practices

To evaluate the impact of trade liberalisation in coffee, it is important to first establish the conditions of trade under the former system of supply management. Between 1962 and 1989 the international coffee market was regulated through a global coffee cartel, the International Coffee Organisation (ICO). The ICO featured broad and inclusive membership of coffee producing and consuming countries and produced a series of 'International Coffee Agreements' (ICAs), sanctioned under the Havana Charter provisions for International Commodity Agreements. While these agreements continue to be negotiated to this day, they now focus on collaboration around aspects such as marketing and research, having long abandoned the economic measures through which they regulated coffee supply and thereby prices for almost 30 years. The key devices used to regulate the coffee market during the ICO's heyday were export quotas and price controls, whereby the ICO worked to stabilise prices to an 'agreed range'[3] by attempting to ensure that coffee supply did not outstrip consumer demand (ICO, 2007a). By all accounts, this system of supply management was relatively successful in its mandate.

Figure 3.1 is based on the ICO composite indicator price, which provides an overall benchmark for the price of green coffee of all major origins and type. The composite indicator price shows that for the period of regulation examined in this graph, 1976–89, a relatively stable price floor was maintained. High prices reflect periods of supply shortage due to environmental factors such as severe frosts in major producing countries (see Talbot, 2004 for a discussion of this). The graph also illustrates how sharply coffee prices fell in the wake of the post-1989 transition to a free market in coffee. The timing of this price collapse directly mirrors the collapse of the ICO regime and the accompanying introduction of trade liberalisation in the coffee trade. Importantly, despite a recent jump in prices from 2006, there has been a generally lower price floor since the abandonment of regulation. Across the board, it's also clear that there is high price volatility in coffee, including a very dramatic dip in prices again from 2011.

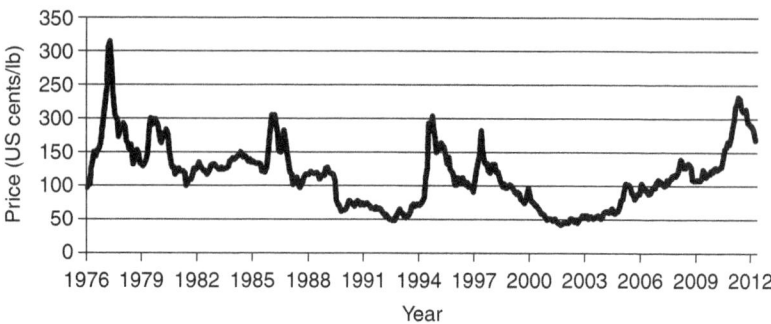

Figure 3.1   The Composite Indicator Price[a] (1976–2012)
Note:
[a] The ICO Composite Indicator Price is calculated with 15 per cent Colombian Milds, 30 per cent Other Milds, 20 per cent Brazilian Naturals and 35 per cent Robustas.
Sources: ICO (2007b, 2010b, 2010c, 2012).

The ability of the ICA regime to maintain price levels through supply management came at a commercial cost for both producing and consuming countries. For example, the ICO regime hid the fact that there remained a duality in the coffee market, with a market for members, and a black market for non-member countries, into which member countries sold excess stock at lower than regulated prices (Talbot, 2004, p. 78). Considering that quota allocations were largely politically negotiated, this meant that there were differences in the revenues producing countries could get, depending on their differential access to the members market and the higher price within, and to low-priced non-member markets. One of the benefits of trade liberalisation in coffee, for both producers who had been marginalised under the ICO regime and traders generally, was that the market did become a level playing field, at least in terms of coffee availability and prices. Essentially, there were two outcomes. First, new varieties and qualities could be traded that were previously restricted because of quotas, and indeed producing countries were no longer limited in their exports. The rise of Brazilian exports and the entry of Vietnam (ICO, 2007c), which quickly became a major player, attest to this. Second, everyone was paying the same, generally very low prices for their coffee.

Indeed, the ICO regime did not necessarily leave a legacy of golden years against which a free trade regime would always pale in comparison. Rather, its success hid deep inequities and produced an oversupply in coffee stocks which led to an instant price collapse once trade barriers were lifted. A mass flooding of the market occurred, whereby a peak in production by coffee producing countries and the dumping of huge quantities of stocks occurred simultaneously. The general downward trend in coffee prices, compared to the levels maintained during the cartel era, however, cannot be attributed to a spillover effect from the former regulatory regime. The period approximately between 1998 and 2005 is renowned as the worst collapse in coffee prices in 100 years. Referred to as the 'coffee crisis', it signified a price collapse, which was worse and longer than that following the end of regulation. Further analysis also shows that since the demise of the ICO regulatory regime, the equity in value distribution has shifted even further away from producing countries.

Value distribution in the coffee market

Income realised from the coffee market can also be analysed by assessing value distributed along the production to retail chain. As the market price shifts, one might expect that producers' prices and retail prices will follow. A lower price on the market, after all, should be passed on in savings to the consumer, and a higher price on the market, equally, should be passed on to the grower. Nonetheless in the last 30 odd years, retail prices in general have stayed relatively steady. So in fact, the key factor behind changes in value distribution for coffee can only partly be attributed to changes in retail prices. Figure 3.2 compares grower prices, market prices and retail prices for selected markets. It shows that additional value on the consumption end of the chain has been achieved not so much by increasing retail prices, but simply by reaping the rewards of lower market prices. Within the 'consumption end' there are of course the various stages of importing, roasting and retail to account for (as well as associated costs); however, it is difficult to get price information on importing and roasting and it is also difficult to say how value is distributed between these different processes. Figure 3.3, however, which is based on analysis by Talbot (2004), does take into account transportation costs and reinforces the view that value distribution has tipped in favour of consuming interests since trade liberalisation took hold. This huge anomaly between value realised in the production end of the marketing chain and the consumption end of the marketing chain for coffee warrants a closer look at 'players' in the coffee market.

Smallholder producers pitted against large multinationals

Historically, the relationship between production and consumption in the coffee marketing chain reads somewhat like the story of 'David

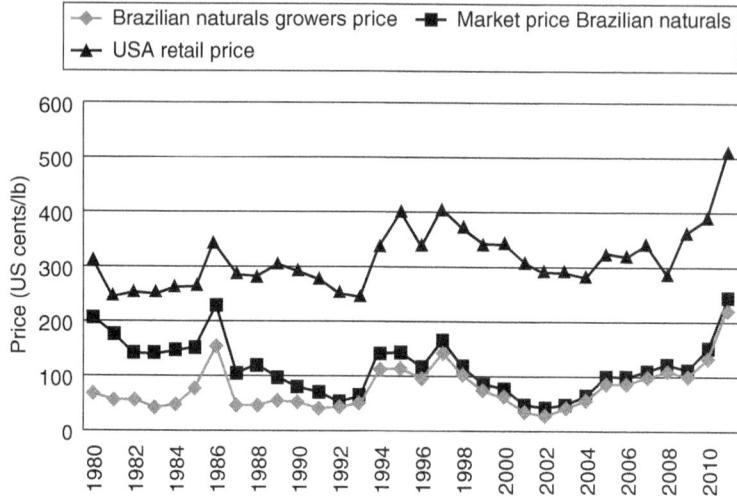

Figure 3.2 US retail price, Brazilian market and producers price (1976–2012)
Sources: ICO (2007b, 2007d, 2010b, 2010c, 2012).

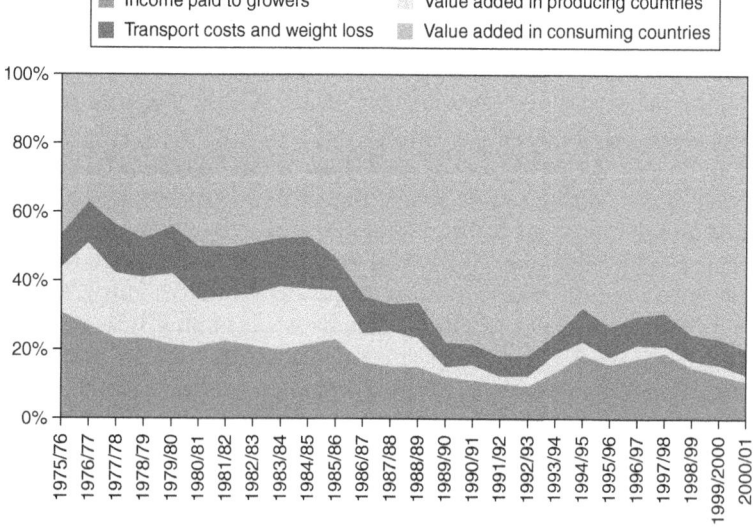

Figure 3.3 Value distribution in the coffee market (1975–2000)
Source: Talbot (2004, pp. 167–8).

and Goliath'. It is a story *literally* of very small interests (individual farmers cultivating smallholdings of less than five hectares typically) pitted against the interests of global enterprise. Before the advent of trade liberalisation, smallholders were somewhat buffered from the consumer market and the big players that dominate consumption in coffee. Generally, they were represented by national 'marketing boards' that bought and sold smallholder coffee. Slob (2006, 129) explains that producers' prices were often fixed by the marketing boards, either on a monthly or yearly basis, whereby producers were largely protected from price volatility. However, the one buffer and locus of power in the governance of the chain which producing countries and smallholder producers had within their countries, the marketing boards, were dissolved through the efforts of the IMF and World Bank. Slob (2006, p. 129) notes that in the 1980s and 90s, '[u]nder pressure from the World Bank and the IMF . . . most marketing boards were dissolved and export taxes were abolished'. Fitter and Kaplinksy (2001, 14) argue that coffee producers have diminished bargaining power by 'sell[ing] atomistically into the commodity markets' as a result. So where does the 'locus of power' in the coffee marketing chain lie now?

The production side of the coffee chain is dominated by smallholder producers who have limited capacity for value-added production let alone to respond to market signals and reduce or shift out of coffee production when prices are low. Historically, labour mobilisation in coffee production has shifted from early models of slave labour to transitional models of coerced labour to, from the end of the nineteenth century, the mix of smallholder and wage-labour production we have today (Daviron and Ponte, 2005, p. 63). This has implications for producer access to higher value activities within the coffee sector. Daviron and Ponte (2005, 66) explain that 'the "peasantisation" of coffee cultivation was accompanied by disintegration of the value chain', as smallholder producers generally do not have the capacity to process their coffee beans and are restricted to low-value activities. However, the introduction of accessible processing technology – the handpulper – has meant that smallholders now are typically able to process their coffee harvests to at least the 'parchment' stage (Daviron and Ponte, 2005, p. 67), which permits storing of the coffee bean without spoiling and attracts a slightly higher price than coffee cherries.[4] On the whole, however, higher value processing has become divorced from production, leaving smallholder producers – who represent the bulk of coffee producers – with limited capacity to achieve higher incomes from their coffee crops.

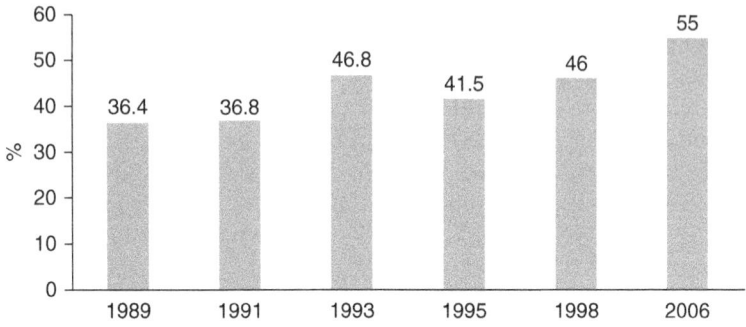

Figure 3.4   Market share of the top five coffee traders (selected years)
Sources: Adapted from Ponte (2001, p. 16), Newman (2009, p. 544) and Fitter and Kaplinsky (2001, p. 79).

The free market logic assumes producer capacity to respond to market signals – for example, low or high prices – with appropriate shifts in production. However, the capacity of coffee producers to do this is inhibited by a range of factors. Coffee is a relatively permanent crop. It takes several years to establish a coffee crop, making it impossible to move in and out of coffee production quickly, or indeed at all (Payer, 1975, p. 155; see also Lewin, Giovannucci and Varangis, 2004, p. 4). While coffee is traditionally shade-grown, which means that it can be intercropped permitting diversified production, modernisation of coffee production has led to the rise of 'sun coffee' or mono-cropping in many origins, which translates into an increased dependence on coffee (Giovanucci and Koekoek, 2003, p. 51). Moreover, diversifying or shifting production into new crops is further complicated by two key factors: producers typically have limited skills and often do not have sufficient funds or the technical support to shift their production into new crops (Robbins, 1995, pp. 97, 227). In contrast, we can observe increasing concentration and vertical integration of value-added activities on the consumption side of the coffee trade.

Both the international trading and roasting activities in the coffee market, are concentrated in the hands of a mere few multinational companies. Figure 3.4 shows the market share of the top five traders in selected years (the traders are not named as the names have changed considerably over the years, by virtue of takeovers and rebranding). This shows that the market share of just a few traders increased from just over 36 per cent in 1989 to 55 per cent in 2006. In an analysis of value distribution in the coffee market, Slob (2006, pp. 129–30) found that the leading coffee traders also held a sizeable stake in the exporting industry of developing countries as well as across all the major producing regions.

The roasting market is also controlled by a few large multinational corporations who are highly influential across the marketing chain. Gresser and Tickell (2002, p. 25) explain that the 'main roasters . . . are giants in the coffee world and shape its retail market'. In 2000, the top five roasters accounted for 44 per cent of the global market (Gresser and Tickell, 2002, p. 25). By 2006, this grew to 46 per cent (Newman, 2009, p. 545). These corporations own well-known major brands including, Nescafé (Nestlé), Maxwell House and Starbucks (Kraft Foods), Folgers and Millstone (Procter & Gamble), and Douwe Egberts and Hills Bros (Sara Lee) (Slob, 2006, p. 130). Effectively, these large roasting MNCs have asserted themselves in both the roasting and retailing of coffee by producing major retail brands.

This discussion highlights the deep inequities in the global coffee market. This further highlights how problematic the comparative advantage thesis is, given its assumptions that economic actors operate on a relatively level playing field in their interactions in the global marketplace. Certainly the coffee case study illustrates the weak position that marginalised producer's hold, relative to that of large corporate entities. Whether due to the operation of free trade in theory or in practice, the realities that producers confront signal the need for major reform in the global trade regime.

Conclusion

The evaluation in this chapter, with comparisons to the lessons of the regulatory era, shows that under free market arrangements there have been significant shifts in the rules and conditions of trade for developing countries. A range of often contradictory regulatory pressures has continued to marginalise developing countries and their agricultural producers. While the Havana Charter interpretation of the treatment of agriculture post-Bretton Woods could have produced a free trade system, which at least recognised the special importance of and problems afflicting trade in agricultural commodities, GATT/WTO and World Bank/IMF interpretation of free trade in agriculture has led to an uneven treatment of agriculture, in which developing countries are marginalised. The World Bank/IMF push to liberalise developing-country markets has left producing countries stripped of the protection of their marketing boards, which in the coffee market helped to buffer smallholder producers against the power of MNCs in the consuming countries. In the study of coffee, it is clear that coffee has presented declining terms of trade, suggesting that other types of exports or even domestic enterprise might offer better long-term opportunities for smallholder coffee producers. Further, the progressive depression of prices and collapse of supports for smallholder producers show that a free trade regime has not so far demonstrated a commitment to production interests in developing countries, and especially those of smallholder producers.

4
The Birth of a Movement and Trade Alternative

Fair Trade has its origins in a significantly distinct and diverse style of engagement with Southern producers, which is largely attributed to the work of Alternative Trade Organisations (ATOs). In recent years, ATOs began identifying as Fair Trade Organisations (FTOs). They operate as socially motivated business entities that are active in international trade by creating an alternative network of exchange, dedicated to enhancing the development prospects of marginalised producers in developing countries. In this articulation of Fair Trade, trade as a process (reflected in the structures and networks of participating businesses), is emphasised.

Today, the umbrella term 'Fair Trade' is understood primarily as a labelling venture associated with Fairtrade-labelled products. This is largely due to the phenomenal growth of Fairtrade-labelled products, which has created a niche in the mainstream market and has been remarkably successful in mainstreaming the concept of Fair Trade itself. The premise of Fairtrade labelling as a mainstream strategy largely relies on the participation of conventional commercial businesses, which typically only commit a small portion of their business to Fairtrade-labelled products. This development has effectively brought Fairtrade to a crossroads, where the movement of activists and ethical businesses within which it was originally conceived must weigh up the opportunities to increase Fair Trade markets through a Fairtrade product model over the potential dilution of Fair Trade values, which a departure from the Fair Trade business model may signify.

This chapter will begin by addressing the confusion presented by the terms 'Fair Trade' and 'alternative trade', noting that there has been an evolution in the terminology used to describe organisations that conduct Fair Trade. The argument is put forward that despite significant overlaps in terms and activities, alternative trade appropriately describes a distinct niche of activity in the Fair Trade sector and it allows for a clearer distinction between a Fairtrade product model which sanctions the participation of conventional commercial businesses (Fairtrade labelling), and a Fair Trade business model (the ambit of alternative or Fair Trade organisations) which arguably provides an applied and *oppositional* model to the conduct and networks of conventional corporate actors. Further, analysis of the opportunities offered in alternative trade networks, comprising important links and partnerships between ATOs and NGOs, indicate unique opportunities for producers who participate in these networks, not least the opportunity to escape the commodity focus of production that characterises trade in both the conventional trade market but also the Fairtrade-labelled market within.

Alternative trade and Fair Trade: Is there a difference?

Since early efforts to liberalise trade, critics have questioned the fairness of both free trade principles and practices. In the context of North–South trade relations, this was heightened with the extension of a free trade model to agriculture in the mid-1990s. Yet, does alternative trade set different standards for engagement with producers than those sanctioned in the conventional market? While the word 'alternative' is all but lost as a label for ethical trading schemes,[1] alternative trade arguably remains as a model of Fair Trade which strongly departs from both free trade principles and practices and also today's more popularised Fairtrade-labelling model.

Origins of fair trade in alternative trade

The language of 'alternative trade' has long been abandoned, yet contemporary Fair Trade campaigns and markets can trace their origins to this earlier push for an alternative system of exchange. Fair Trade hails back to the creation of an alternative trade market, whereby trade was re-crafted as a socially embedded process, led by the values and activities promoted by pioneering NGOs and their alternative trade offspring (ATOs). The first phase of alternative trade activity is typically traced to the activities of NGOs importing from marginalised producers in the South: first observed in the US in the 1940s (Redfern and Snedker, 2002, p. 5) and in Europe in the 1950s (Giovannucci and Koekoek, 2003, p. 38). This strategy of engagement became more organised through the creation of a new and dedicated business model – the ATO – when Oxfam UK founded the first ATO in 1964 (IFAT, 2006) as its 'trading subsidiary' (Redfern and Snedker, 2002, p. 5). Moving beyond an early focus on political solidarity to a concern with unequal exchange, NGOs quickly refocussed the mandate of alternative trade, emphasising trade reform as an engine for development under the motto – 'trade, not aid' (Renard, 2003, p. 89).

In contrast to the emphasis on principles of freedom in conventional trade, the alternative trade model wedded itself to principles of fairness in exchange. In his pioneering book *Fair Trade: Reform and Realities in the International Trading System*, Michael Barratt Brown (1993, p. 156) defined alternative trade as 'a system of trade in which the partners seek deliberately to establish a more equal basis of exchange between the First and the Third Worlds'. By directly linking producers and consumers, alternative trade is argued to foster 'a greater understanding among consumers of the need of the producers for support for their independent development' (Barratt Brown, 1993, p. 156). In principle, ATOs challenged the logic that competition should determine prices with concern that prices should reflect basic needs and support sustainable livelihoods. This was clearly articulated by the then International Federation for Alternative Trade (IFAT in Renard, 2003, p. 89)[2] which argued that '[a]lternative trade operates under a different set of values and objectives than traditional trade, putting people and their well-being and preservation of the natural environment before the pursuit of profit'. Further, NGOs like Oxfam objected to free trade practices, which were and continue to be understood as fundamentally 'rigged' by many. Oxfam ran a 'Make Trade Fair' campaign, whereby it argued that trade reform alone could 'lift millions out of poverty' through 'changes to trade rules that are rigged by powerful multinational companies and rich countries in their favour' (Oxfam, 2006).

Indeed, from the outset, alternative trade positioned itself as opposed to both the principles and practices that characterise exchange between North and South, and accordingly the types of business models that operate within the conventional trade system. It is on this point that the trading activities and networks of these alternative businesses remain well defined as alternative, not only to distinguish them from the values and activities of conventional commercial businesses but also to distinguish them from the networks of Fairtrade labelling which invite conventional businesses to participate.

ATOs: Dual social and economic role

Today, ATOs are typically known as FTOs (see Krier, 2005, p. 22).[3] They continue to offer a markedly different model of exchange to that which typifies Fairtrade-labelling networks and the conventional businesses which these invite into their ranks. While the obvious point of difference may be that traditional alternative traders today call themselves 'Fair Trade', not 'Fairtrade', the difference actually goes much deeper. The ATO business model bridges the divide between a socially motivated or development organisation, and an economic or commercial business entity. Barratt Brown (1993, p. 163) argues that ATOs occupy a unique role as a 'middleman' distinct 'from the sharks, coyotes and piranhas' which traditionally occupy the commercial marketplace. Accordingly, the ATO assumes a number of unique functions and characteristics distinct from conventional actors motivated by profit as their bottom line. Barratt Brown (1993, pp. 163–4) described the ATOs distinct characteristics as follows:

- Identify producer groups in developing countries seeking to connect with markets in the North.
- Provide producers with necessary commercial information such as that pertaining to markets and relevant product standards.
- Are willing to not only undertake but also essentially pursue commercially risky business. ATOs assume a high financial burden through providing producers with start-up financing and also paying higher prices than those commanded in the commercial marketplace. But they also need to ensure that their products are competitive in the market and as such walk a very fine line in terms of their commercial viability. Barratt Brown (1993, p. 163) notes that 'the aim is to pay as much as possible, not as little as possible, to the producer, yet at the same time to offer goods on the market at competitive prices or at prices that are acceptable to consumers because they know that the extra they pay is going to those that are in need'.
- Provide a public relations role for producers. Essentially, 'ATOs wish to influence consumer demand, not so much towards the product they are marketing and away from someone else's, as towards Third World products as a whole and, more important, towards a different attitude to international trade relations' (Barratt Brown, 1993, p. 164). In this respect, ATOs are not simply marketing products, but rather a whole philosophy about business conduct, the environment in which businesses operate, and the producers and consumers for which they provide the key interface.

A useful way in which to capture this multifarious and social mandate of ATOs is to examine the WFTOs' guiding principles for its members.

The WFTOs accreditation of ATOs demonstrates the importance of social principles to ATOs. The WFTO comprises a broad membership[4] and its responsibilities and authority as an international association are extensive. In its monitoring role,[5] the WFTO works as an accrediting agency, providing permission to use the 'WFTO logo' to 'organisations who demonstrate a 100% commitment to fair trade in all their business activities' (WFTO, 2011). This assessment is based on compliance with the WFTOs '10 Principles of Fair Trade' (WFTO, 2010a).[6] This is an important aspect of how ATOs develop their reputations as socially committed businesses. Indeed, the international principles developed by the WFTO, as applied to organisations spanning production to consumption in alternative trade networks, clearly demonstrate the social role of ATOs.

The first principle requires that 'poverty reduction through trade' is central to an organisation's objectives and that the organisation 'supports marginalised small producers' (WFTO, 2010a). Infused into the economic objectives contained in this principle are the social/development outcomes, which ATOs are expected to deliver. Principle nine requires the promotion and advocacy of Fair Trade, above and beyond the requirement placed on conventional businesses, which are typically not expected to support a social cause as part of their business model. This principle requires that 'the organisation raises awareness of the aims of Fair Trade and of the need for greater justice in world trade through Fair Trade' (WFTO, 2010a). Arguably, the social mandate of ATOs is mutually supportive with the economic objective of expanding the Fair Trade market (the promotion of Fair Trade is good for producers supplying this market, but it also makes business sense for the ATOs operating in it); underlining the dual social and economic roles of ATOs. Principle four requires organisations to pay a 'fair' price to producers, which 'can also be sustained by the market' (WFTO, 2010a). Here, a fair price must ensure the 'provision of socially acceptable remuneration (in the local context) considered by producers themselves to be fair' (WFTO, 2010a). The payment of a fair price, according to WFTO principles, must take into account the economic dictates of the market and the social requirements of the producers. Principle three on Trading Practices requires that an 'organisation trades with concern for the social, economic and environmental well-being of marginalised producers and does not maximise profit at their expense' (WFTO, 2010a). Thus, organisations must not only be socially and economically minded in their engagement with producers, but also forfeit the profit motive that drives conventional businesses to ensure that no surpluses are accrued at the cost of producers. A commitment to principles such as transparency and accountability (principle two), outlawing of child labour and forced labour (principle five), non-discrimination (in principle six), safe working conditions (principle seven), capacity building (principle eight) and concern for the environment (principle ten), further exemplifies the overarching requirement that members of the WFTO are socially engaged and conscious entities, not just economically driven businesses.

One of the important devices by which the social values of ATOs are ensured, so that values such as those mandated by the WFTO for its membership can be upheld, is the financial structure of an ATO or that which frames an ATO/NGO partnership with respect to joint projects or objectives. For example, Twin Trading (a UK-based ATO which primarily trades coffee) gives all of its profits to its NGO arm Twin (by covenant), while Twin dedicates the majority of its work to supporting the coffee producers that supply Twin Trading (Twin and Twin Trading, 2005). These kinds of financial arrangements cement an ongoing commitment to social goals in the economic activities and design of the ATO.

While the range of ATOs are diverse (in terms of their activities, partnerships and size), a common objective binds them: support of, and engagement in, Fair Trade. This in turn means a common objective to support and engage with marginalised producers through alternative trade, which platforms a qualitatively (socially and ethically) different process for economic exchange with southern producers. A clearer understanding of the role and features of alternative trade, especially in terms of the opportunities offered to marginalised producers, becomes easier to trace when looking at the profile and activities of different ATOs.

ATOs: The consumption end of the trading chain

At the consumption end of the trading chain, ATOs vary in their specialisation (e.g. processing or marketing functions and product specialisation), scale of operation, and coverage of different consumer markets. An ATO may be an ethical importer, manufacturer or retail outlet (traditionally called 'Worldshop') working in or across countries. Smaller ATOs are often dedicated to one product, one processing function and one consumer market, with perhaps some greater coverage in one or more of these areas (e.g. multiple products or the undertaking of roasting and importing in the case of coffee). However, it is the larger ATOs, or herein 'super-ATOs', whose role and impact are more difficult to pin down, due to the multifunctional nature of their activities and their networks. Yet these super-ATOs often account for the largest slice of the ATO pie, being the biggest players in alternative marketing chains. They also play a pioneering role in broadening the Fair Trade market, including new ventures such as Fairtrade labelling.

This section examines the opportunities that the multimillion-dollar Fair Trade importing industry presents to marginalised producers, primarily in Europe. Specifically, this section examines the social mandate of leading ATOs operating in highly competitive commercial environments through a profile of two major ATO/NGO partnerships based in the UK. Each of these is international in the scale of its operations and also fulfils a range of roles in alternative trade networks. Finally, the collaborative strategy of branding products, which these super-ATOs have employed in an attempt to mainstream Fair Trade products, is examined. It becomes clear that ATOs are understood as not only alternative through their values and mode of operation, but often equally so by their development of complex and typically insular alternative trade networks (with the exception of mainstreaming efforts), which provide unique opportunities, in terms of producer support.

Importing ATOs

The major European importing organisations represented by EFTA present something of a challenge to the characteristic typology of ATOs, due to either their dedicated market coverage or specialisation. EFTA currently has a membership of ten Fair Trade importers across nine European countries and many of these organisations are multimillion-dollar ventures that test the classification of being merely importers (Boonman et al., 2011, p. 29). Drawing on 2006 data from the last comprehensive study of this sector, it is clear that across Europe, the biggest Fair Trade importers dominate the European Fair Trade market. The top three accounted for 49 per cent of the market, while the top 13 accounted for 78 per cent of the market (Krier, 2008, pp. 36, 137).[7] As a comparison and with similar results, the top three importing ATOs in North America and the Pacific Rim accounted for 64 per cent of the market (Krier, 2008, pp. 38, 139).[8]

The European super-ATOs are part of a multimillion-dollar industry, which has demonstrated high growth in recent years, indicating that the European alternative trade industry, in terms of market opportunities for producers, may still offer significant growth in the future. Table 4.1 shows that between 2000 and 2004, the number of ATO importers in Europe doubled, with a total 27 per cent increase in the number of players between 2004 and 2007. During this time the turnover of the biggest organisations increased dramatically (by a remarkable 95 per cent), accounting for more than half of the turnover of all ATO

Table 4.1   Fair Trade market in Europe (2000–7)[a]: Importing organisations

Year	2000	2004	2007	% change
Turnover of biggest[b] importing organisations	€92.7m	€167.5m	€325.719m	+251
Total number of ATO importing organisations in Europe	97	200	254	+162
Total turnover of importing organisations in Europe	€118.9m	€243.3m	€422.225m	+255
Education/PR marketing of importing organisations in Europe	€5.6m	€11.4m	n/a[c]	+104

Note:
[a]Data provided by Krier (2008, p. 11) compares figures from her 2001, 2005 and 2007 reports. For instance, the 2005 data generally refers to fiscal year 2004, but in some cases to fiscal year 2003; however, a breakdown of where this applies to the data is not given in the report.
[b]'Biggest' is defined by Krier as attaining an annual turnover greater than €10 million. In 2007 this refers to 13 importing organisations; the 2000 and 2004 data is based on the seven biggest importing organisations at that time.
[c]Insufficient data available.
Sources: Krier (2005, p. 9; 2008, p. 11).

importing organisations in Europe by 2007. It is difficult to provide a comparison with Fairtrade labelling, partly due to availability of data but particularly because Fairtrade-labelled products, are also sold within the networks of ATOs (this creates significant overlaps in the data pertaining to ATO activity and that pertaining to labelling activity).

ATOs also make an important contribution in terms of the education of consumers. By promoting and marketing the development and expansion of Fair Trade, they underscore the social mandate of these unique businesses with the aim to increase opportunities for producers to supply Fair Trade products. Investment in education especially, distinguishes ATOs from conventional businesses, as this expense is primarily cause related, serving the purpose of advancing greater awareness and support of Fair Trade. This reinforces Barratt Brown's (1993) characterisation of ATOs which argues that the PR and marketing activities of ATOs are key to ATOs aims: to create a more supportive trade environment for marginalised producers, and more generally to promote an alternative trade philosophy. Yet arguably these expenses also serve a 'business' purpose, insofar as growing support for Fair Trade as a movement will also positively impact Fair Trade sales. The end result, either way, is to garner the support of consumers, which will hopefully translate into expanding the market for, and thus producer opportunities to supply, Fair Trade products. Table 4.1 shows that expenditure across education, PR and marketing activities doubled for importing organisations in a four-year period from €5.6 million in 2000 to €11.4 million in 2004, compared to the significantly lower levels of investment and expenditure growth for Fairtrade labelling in the same period (€3.5 million to €5.1 million; Krier, 2008, p. 11). In this respect ATOs still lead the way, in terms of their commitment to, and role in, promoting and advancing Fair Trade principles, businesses and products.

The UK, a particularly well-established and successful Fair Trade market, is described by Krier (2005, p. 66) as having 'probably the most dynamic Fair Trade structures of all European countries'. The case studies examined next are that of Traidcraft plc and its NGO arm, Traidcraft Exchange, as well as Twin Trading and its NGO arm, Twin.[9] These examples will examine the importance and the implications of partnerships with NGOs, as well as strategies not only to mainstream Fair Trade but also to offer producers a measure of ownership over activities in the consumer markets.

UK super-ATOs: Traidcraft

The example of Traidcraft exemplifies the unique opportunities offered to producers by an NGO–ATO partnership. Traidcraft is described as 'the largest traditional Fair Trade organisation in terms of staff numbers and product range' in the UK (Krier, 2008, p. 103). However, in terms of its impact on producers from the South, it is best examined in the context and scope of both its ATO and NGO activities. Table 4.2 captures the key commonalities and differences between the two partner organisations, identifying key roles, strategies and impacts.

Traidcraft has a unique structure, as it 'is both a commercial trading company (Traidcraft plc) and a non-profit organisation (Traidcraft Exchange) (Humphrey, 2000, p. 3). The duo was founded by Traidcraft Foundation, which holds a guardian share in the ATO arm, Traidcraft plc, with the NGO arm, Traidcraft Exchange, a subsidiary of the Foundation (Traidcraft Foundation, 2012, pp. 4–5). Together, these organisations are committed to a mission to 'fight poverty through trade pioneering, practising and promoting approaches to trade that help poor people in developing countries to transform their lives' (Traidcraft Foundation, 2012, p. 3). Essentially, the Traidcraft ATO and NGO work as a partnership dedicated to broadly the same principles and objectives.

Table 4.2 Traidcraft: Organisational features and marketing networks

	Traidcraft plc	Traidcraft Exchange
Governance/ stakeholders	Traidcraft Foundation holds the Guardian Share and has the power to veto appointments to the ATOs Board of Directors	Subsidiary of Traidcraft Foundation, which appoints the board of directors
Date established	1979	1986
Key strategies	Trades directly with producers, supports (builds capacity of producers) and influences (campaigns for change in trade) Spends a high portion of the cost of sales in developing countries	Same as Traidcraft plc – to trade (in this case facilitate trade), support and influence
Roles and activities	Importing and retail as well as producer support	Producer Support, campaigning against international trade rules Campaigns and lobbies globally for Fair Trade Works directly with producers to improve capacity and market access Provides support for Traidcraft plc
Product specialisation	Grocery items (e.g. foods and beverages), clothing and craft goods.	Tea, honey, jute and crafts
Major markets	UK (biggest ATO in the UK)	n/a
Growth and turnover	Turnover (£17 million in 2012) and sales have been declining due largely to increasing competition	Income for 2012 was £4.15 million
Where do the profits go?	Profits are invested back into the business to grow its trading activities and impact on producers. It does not fund Traidcraft Exchange	Non-profit

Associate/subsidiary company in coffee	Founding owner of Cafedirect, however, sold its 10% share in 2011	n/a
Producer supports/ joint ventures	Joint venture with Traidcraft Exchange: Producer Support and Innovation Programme	Trade-related development programmes through its Overseas Development Programme, Producer Support and Innovation Programme and Policy and Advocacy Programme
Producer partners	Producers in more than 30 countries across Africa, South Asia, Latin America and Southeast Asia	East Africa and South Asia

Sources: Humphrey (2000, p. 3); Krier (2008, p. 103); Traidcraft (2006; 2009, p. 6; 2012, pp. 4–10, 2 and 78), Traidcraft Exchange (2012, p. 4–5); Traidcraft Foundation (2012, pp. 4–5).

The Traidcraft NGO–ATO duo describes its role as threefold: to benefit producers through *trade*, to *support* people by building their capacity to develop businesses, and to *influence* trading rules and public and political attitudes (Traidcraft, 2006). The two arms of Traidcraft – Traidcraft plc and Traidcraft Exchange – seek to apply a holistic approach to their relationship with producers through direct purchasing on the one hand (via importing by Traidcraft plc) and through supporting producer capacity to engage in and benefit from trade on the other hand (via the support role of Traidcraft Exchange).

While the Traidcraft ATO arm conducts the business of Fair Trade, the NGO arm helps producers to access, and to participate in, Traidcraft's trading activities through provision of support services. Traidcraft Exchange provides supports for producers in the South through its Overseas Development Programme (across East Africa and South Asia) Producer Support and Innovation Programme (providing support to Traidcraft plc's trading partners) and Policy and Advocacy Programme (to exert pressure on companies and governments across the UK and Europe) (through which it provides consultancy services) (Traidcraft Exchange, 2012, pp. 4–5). The ATO-NGO partnership on Fair Trade becomes clear when we examine the rationale for the Producer Support and Innovation Programme. As a joint initiative of Traidcraft Exchange and Traidcraft plc, this programme aims to combine the ATOs knowledge of the trade and the suppliers it works with, with the NGOs 'development and fundraising expertise' (Traidcraft Exchange, 2012, p. 14). They particularly target producers that 'require support beyond what can reasonably be provided through the fair trading relationship' (Traidcraft Exchange, 2012, p. 14). The overarching aim, however, is that these producers become independent over time so that they no longer require additional development support (Traidcraft Exchange, 2012, p. 14). Recent activities include supporting craft and textile producers in Guatemala and ceramic and craft producers in Peru (Traidcraft Exchange, 2012, p. 16).

While Traidcraft plc relies on the activities of its NGO arm for support services to its producer suppliers, there are a number of opportunities it offers its suppliers through a direct trading relationship. Traidcraft, as standard practice, makes a long-term commitment to its producers and aims to support a fair exchange as articulated in its purchasing policies. Traidcraft claims to 'pay prices that enable producers to earn a fair return for their efforts' but also, to provide access to credit and advance payments when required, to make additional premium payments for 'community development' and to advance the proportion of value-added activities taking place in developing countries (Traidcraft, 2005, p. 2). In this respect, Traidcraft plc works towards offering producers a sustained and predictable income. Traidcraft plc also has a policy of boosting the value retained in producing countries by spending a high portion of the 'cost of sales' in developing countries, (Traidcraft, 2009, p. 6).

Just as the support activities of Traidcraft Exchange are extensive, the activities of Traidcraft plc are not limited to importing alone; rather, it provides a variety of retail pathways for producers' products, including Worldshops. Traidcraft retails its Fair Trade products through four key avenues: mail-order catalogues; online shopping; a network of volunteer 'Fairtraders' (who sell Traidcraft products 'in their church, workplace, school, community centre to family, friends and neighbours'); and through retail venues, including Waitrose, Tesco and Booth's supermarkets (Traidcraft, 2004). It could be argued that its mail-order and online retail services create quasi cyber and mail-order Worldshops, while Fairtraders maintain traditional Worldshops in their communities. In addition, Traidcraft has succeeded in mainstreaming its products through commercial retail outlets.

Traidcraft imports a range of food products, but also a diverse range of craft products (see Traidcraft 2012), thus illustrating the dedication of ATOs to production beyond commodities. Examination of Traidcraft is also valuable in illustrating the high level of involvement, from production to sale, which many super-ATOs, through their partnership with ATOs, assume in their relationship with producers. Traidcraft is also an important case study to consider as, in partnership with three other ATOs, it pioneered the first effort by ATOs in Europe to mainstream Fair Trade products, specifically coffee, through Cafédirect (see discussion later in this chapter). One of these partners was Twin Trading.

UK super-ATOs: Twin

Similar to Traidcraft, Twin also operates as an NGO/ATO partnership. Table 4.3 identifies the key roles and activities of the two organisations, and identifies key differences in the work that they do. Like the Traidcraft partnership, Twin focuses on producer support projects while Twin Trading imports directly from producers (Twin and Twin Trading, 2005). Interestingly, 'all profits made by Twin Trading are covenanted to Twin' (Twin and Twin Trading, 2005), confirming the close partnership between these sister organisations. This also ensures that the potential profitability of this ATO as a business venture does not divert its commitment to the development objectives that underpin its social

62

Table 4.3 Twin: Organisational features and marketing networks

	Twin Trading	Twin
Governance/ stakeholders	Twin Trading is a limited company	Twin is a registered charity
Date established	1985	1985
Key strategies	Branding with producer ownership	Aims to support producer capacity to trade especially in coffee
Roles and activities	Active in trade with marginalised producers. Also provides loan finance to producers and facilitates producer access to alternative sources of funding	Producer support role and campaigning to change trade rules
Product specialisation	Traditionally coffee and cocoa but recently added nuts (fiscal year 2004–5)	Supports producers supplying Twin Trading
Major markets	89% of its coffee imports were sourced for Cafédirect in fiscal year 2001–2 but it also supplies a number of other ATOs	n/a
Growth and turnover	Between 1995 and 2005 Twin Trading increased its turnover by 100% and for fiscal year 2011–12 had a turnover of £18.3 million	Income for 2011–12 was £1.3 million
Where do the profits go?	All profits covenanted to Twin (e.g. in fiscal year 2004–5 this amounted to 12% of Twin's total funding) Also in fiscal year 2010–11 £20,000 was donated to Twin	Non-profit
Associate/ subsidiary company in coffee	Associated with, in some cases as shareholder, four Fair Trade brands: Cafédirect, Agrofair UK, Divine Chocolate and Liberation Foods	n/a
Producer supports/joint ventures	n/a	Supports producers that Twin Trading trades with
Producer partners	Working across 18 countries with 50 growers organisations/ approximately 400 000 growers	As above

Sources: Krier (2008, p. 104; Twin (2012); Twin and Twin Trading (2002; 2005, pp. 17–9; 2011, p. 11; 2012, pp. 2 and 10).

mandate. In fact, the synergies between the two organisations are not only financial. Both organisations are committed to supporting marginalised coffee producers. For example, of the turnover Twin Trading realised in the financial year 2001–2, 88 per cent was related to coffee and similarly 70 per cent of Twin's projects were devoted to supporting coffee producers (Twin and Twin Trading, 2002). This alignment in activities continues today.

Both Twin and Twin Trading are also integrated into a broader ATO network, through the strategy of mainstreaming. Twin Trading is associated, in some cases as a shareholder, with a number of Fair Trade brand ATOs: Cafédirect, AgroFair, Liberation Foods and Divine Chocolate (Twin, 2012). In jointly creating Cafédirect, Twin Trading created a commercial coffee brand retail vehicle for its coffee imports, claiming that in fiscal year 2001–2, 89 per cent of the value of its coffee trade 'was sourced on behalf of Cafédirect' (Twin and Twin Trading, 2005). Similarly, in 2011 it became the sole importer for 'Liberation Foods', immediately doubling its nut imports (Twin and Twin Trading, 2012, p. 8). The significance of the Cafédirect mainstreaming strategy to alternative trade networks in coffee is considered next.

Super-ATOs: Strategies to mainstream Fair Trade products

Worldshops are the alternative trade equivalent of what conventional retail spaces, such as supermarkets or department stores, are to the conventional marketplace. Yet sales through Worldshops, now more commonly known as Fair Trade Shops, are diminishing. Already by 2006, Worldshops accounted for a mere 5 per cent of the sales outlets in which Fair Trade products are sold, with the remainder sold in conventional supermarkets (Krier, 2008, pp. 11, 153). This underscores the importance of mainstream strategies within Fair Trade for reaching a wider consumer base. Even before the advent of Fairtrade labelling, ATOs embarked on the challenge of mainstreaming their Fair Trade products, and the first of these ventures was in coffee. This follows an important logic that is also embraced through the promotion of Fairtrade labelling, with Renard (2003, p. 90) explaining that 'it was more profitable to offer the products at places where consumers normally shop: in the large distribution channels. Young (2003, p. 6) identifies two key strategies which were adapted to mainstream Fair Trade: the Cafédirect model, founded by ATOs; and the first labelling initiative (Max Havelaar in 1989; see discussion in Chapter 5).

Table 4.4 examines key features and achievements of the Cafédirect model for mainstreaming coffee. Cafédirect was established in 1991 by

Table 4.4   Cafédirect plc: Organisational features and marketing networks

Governance/ stakeholders	Oxfam, Twin Trading, Equal Exchange and Traidcraft founded the company. Only Oxfam retains it's 10% share holdings today (in addition to some new shareholders). Cafedirect producers own a 5.5% share of the company and together with Oxfam hold Guardians' Share
Date established	1991
Key strategies	Mainstreaming Fairtrade products by creating a commercially competitive brand. Through a 2004 re-structure, Cafedirect reformed as Cafedirect Plc. It now has an NGO partnership with the newly created 'Cafedirect Producers Foundation' (producer owned), which runs its Producer Partnership Programme (PPP)
Roles and activities	Trading company which actively provides support to its producer partners
Product specialisation	Primarily coffee but also tea and cocoa
Major markets	Primary market is the UK
Growth and turnover	Turnover was £13.8 million in 2011
Where do the profits go?	Publicly owned company – dividends to shareholders. However, it also makes significant donations to it's NGO arm – Cafedirect Producers Foundation
Marketing networks	Major trading partnerships with other ATOs
Producer supports/ joint ventures	FLO Pricing policies. Also, the PPP is designed to support Cafédirect suppliers by investing in their businesses
Producer partners	Sources from producers in Latin America, Africa and Asia

Sources: Cafédirect, 2008a, p 18; 2008b, pp. 20–1; 2010a); Cafedirect (2011a, pp. 2–3, 5 and 22), Cafedirect (2011b, p. 11), Cafedirect (2010c, p. 20).

Oxfam, Traidcraft, Equal Exchange and Twin Trading (Cafédirect, 2005). It predates the introduction of Fairtrade labelling in the UK by three years (Cafédirect, 2010a), and today all of its products are 100 per cent Fairtrade certified (Cafédirect, 2010b). Today, Oxfam remains a 10% shareholder and together with Cafedirect Producers Ltd (CPL), which holds 5.5% of ordinary shares, holds a guardian share in the company

(Cafedirect, 2011, p. 5). This guardian share confers a range of rights, including allowing Oxfam and producers to appoint a director to the Board of the company (Cafedirect, 2011, p. 28).

Cafédirect created a Fair Trade brand of coffee, and 'commercial' Fair Trade coffees – like Cafédirect – now account for a significant portion of the UK market, representing '14% of the UK roast and ground coffee market' in 2003 (Young, 2003, pp. 6–7). By February 2005 it had achieved £22.7 million in retail sales for this market and became 'the sixth largest UK coffee brand' (Twin and Twin Trading, 2005, p. 17). This stands to benefit the '40 producers' organisations across 14 countries, encompassing over 260 000 farmers' with which Cafédirect trades (Cafédirect, 2010a). Beyond its impact on the incomes of smallholder coffee producers, through sourcing and marketing coffee (very successfully in the UK), Cafédirect also provides direct support to its suppliers.

One of Cafédirect's key strategies is to trade with as many producer organisations as it can, by creating small partnerships that minimise the chance of producer dependence (Cafédirect, 2006, p. 12). However, it also tries to raise producer independence through its PPP. The programme is designed to support Cafédirect suppliers through 'investments to strengthen the business of suppliers' (Cafédirect, 2006, p. 19). This program is now manged by it's sister NGO, Cafedirect Producers Foundation (see Table 4.4). The program demonstrates the importance of its trade and support roles to Cafédirect.

Similarly, Divine Chocolate (of which Twin Trading is a part owner) creates a Fair Trade brand for chocolate, whereby it 'is a limited joint venture company purposely set up for the mainstreaming of Fairtrade chocolate in the UK' (Ronchi, 2002, p. 18). It began with two chocolate bars, Divine and Dubble, which quickly grew in distribution across major retail outlets in the UK (see Ronchi, 2002, p. 19). While labelling is an important and growing avenue for the commercial retailing of Fair Trade products, the creation of commercially competitive Fair Trade brands like Cafédirect and Divine Chocolate exemplify how innovative ATOs have been in creating space in the conventional market for the products of their producer partners. This, without sacrificing the traditional strategy of building and maintaining a fair business reputation, as ATO brands provide a mainstream strategy where the integrity of the (ATO) businesses behind the products remains as important as the reputation of the products themselves.

Mainstreaming has served as an important strategy for ATOs to reach a wider consumer base. Even so, success in mainstreaming has primarily been achieved for food and beverage products such as coffee, and today has largely become the domain of Fairtrade labelling organisations. This is not surprising as ATO networks are uniquely positioned to offer opportunities to producers, not only in agricultural commodities (which dominate the product range available in Fairtrade labelling) but also handicrafts. Thus, unlike Fairtrade labelling which reinforces the trend to predominantly source agricultural commodities from developing countries, as typical in the conventional market, ATOs continue to pioneer diversification of production for marginalised producers. Despite this, handicraft products are increasingly marginalised in the Fair Trade market, suggesting further work needs to be done to strengthen the position of these producers.

Handicraft products accounted for 80 per cent of products sold in 1992, a trend which was reversed ten years later in 2002 when agricultural products coveted 70 per cent of the Fair Trade pie over the 26 per cent accounted for by handicrafts (Nicholls and Opal sourced in Boonman et al., 2011). This suggests the need for a new mainstreaming strategy to again elevate the position of handicrafts, which Joan Karanja, Director of the Producer Association for Africa – Cooperation for Fair Trade in Africa (COFTA) – claims 'is the trade of the poor [as] . . . [T]hey don't have the land to produce food' (Boonman et al., 2011, p. 37). While the Fairtrade labelling model (predicated on certification of uniform products) lacks the capacity to certify diverse products like handicrafts, the WFTO is working on creating a label (Hutchens, 2009, p. 77). EFTA estimates significant growth in this sector if such a label is created (Boonman et al., 2011, p. 23). A push for developments such as these underscores the importance of ensuring that Fair Trade evolves to meet the needs of the marginalised producers it seeks to represent. Hearing the voices of producers, such as that of producer representative Joan Karanja, is thus crucial to ensure that Fair Trade remains relevant.

ATO networks and the voice of producer partners

In most of the literature, be it that of ATOs, NGOs or labelling organisations, the producers with whom these organisations engage are typically referred to as producer partners, suggesting an equality in their status and partnership in their working relationship. Certainly, marginalised producers are clearly the key link and focus in Fair Trade activity. Campaigns to change global trading rules are undertaken on their behalf, NGO projects in the South often focus on building the capacity of producers for community development and/or trade, and ATOs such as ATO importers and Worldshops owe their existence to the desire in the Fair Trade community to market and sell products from the South on fairer terms than those perceived to exist in conventional trading markets. Some important aspects of the impact of alternative trade on producers have been explored in previous sections, including an evaluation of opportunities in alternative trade markets; the scope and scale of these markets; potential future prospects, with reference to the commitment of ATOs to educating consumers and growing alternative trade markets; as well as the opportunities in terms of additional supports offered by ATO–NGO partnerships in alternative trade. This section will assess how producers are represented in the formal regional producer networks for alternative trade.

Regional associations: Formal producer networks in alternative trade

From an institutional point of view, the producer partners in ATO networks also have their own avenues for collective representation, through dedicated and specialised regional associations. These associations cover WFTO producer members across Asia and the Pacific, Africa and Latin America, and fall under the institutional umbrella of the WFTO, as 'WFTO regional chapters' (WFTO, 2010b). Indeed, the Cooperation for Fair Trade in Africa (COFTA, 2006) claims that regional networks were created by the WFTO 'to address the particular needs of specific regions around the world', and it was on this premise that COFTA was established in 2004. COFTA (2012a) sees itself as 'working with disadvantaged grass root producers to eliminate poverty through Fair Trade'. This highlights the importance of producer organisations, and effective representation of producer priorities and needs (especially regionally), to the international alternative trade community at large, and to producing organisations regionally.

The coverage of these regional associations can be quite extensive. COFTA (2012b) currently represents 70 member organisations spanning 17 African countries. It also has individual national networks in Zimbabwe, Kenya, Rwanda, Swaziland, Tanzania and Senegal (COFTA, 2012c). The Latin American producer network, WFTO Latin America (formerly IFAT LA), represents 52 organisations spanning 13 countries across Latin America (IFAT LA, 2010). The Asian producer association, WFTO Asia (formerly the Asia Fair Trade Forum – AFTF), also has an extensive reach in its region representing 90 member organisations across 14 countries (WFTO Asia, 2010). The European producer association, WFTO Europe (formerly IFAT Europe) represents 52 members across 15 countries (WFTO Europe, 2010). Meanwhile, WFTO Pacific represents countries across North America and the Pacific, including producer organisations, support organisations, national networks and individual associates (WFTO Pacific, 2010). There are currently 34 members spanning Canada, Australia, Japan, the US, New Zealand and the Pacific islands (currently only PNG) (WFTO Pacific, 2010).

While these formal networks provide an important platform for producers to access and influence the institutional networks that frame alternative trade activities, it is predominantly the relationships and networks that producer organisations gain with ATOs in consumer countries, which build their experience of alternative trade networks. These will be explored in Chapter 7 through a case study of coffee production and trade.

Conclusion

The defining attributes of alternative exchange are best understood through an examination of the characteristic business values and networks of ATOs. Essentially, ATOs operate as both socially motivated and economically driven business entities that seek to implement these values in their organisational structures and in their trading networks. ATOs individually attempt to implement business values that support the development goals of the producers they trade with, and further, as a trading network they typically preference trade with other ATOs that share these values. While Fairtrade labelling seeks to engage conventional commercial businesses, ATOs typically try to ensure that Fair Trade principles are honoured by all businesses engaged in the hence aptly coined 'alternative trade networks', with the exception of mainstreaming strategies where conventional retail outlets are sought. As such, ATOs model an alternative to the modus operandi of conventional businesses and indeed the very workings of the commercial marketplace. This model further sets ATOs apart from Fairtrade labelling, which by engaging conventional businesses runs the risk of reinforcing and indeed endorsing these market actors. In addition, unlike Fairtrade labelling, ATOs continue to push for product diversification beyond the commodity trap that continues to characterise production across both Fairtrade labelling and the conventional market. While the limitations of alternative markets have warranted the creation of mainstreaming strategies, which ATOs themselves have actively pioneered, it is useful to consider what has been gained and what has been lost in moving from a Fair Trade business model to a Fairtrade product model. This is the concern of the following chapter.

5
Fairtrade: Peeling Back the Label

Fairtrade labelling merges its products onto the shelves of mainstream retail outlets by employing a hallmark device which distinguishes it from other Fair Trade models: product assurance. Fairtrade labelling does not vouch for the general business practices of the companies that trade and sell Fairtrade-labelled products, but rather it vouches for those associated with the trade of Fairtrade-labelled products. While ATOs make promises about their general business practices, the Fairtrade label simply promises to provide producers with better conditions relating to the trade of the products they sell as Fairtrade. Indeed, this is the key message provided by the Fairtrade label, conveyed to consumers every time they purchase a Fairtrade product: 'FAIRTRADE guarantees a better deal for Third World Producers'.[1] However, the device of product assurance in Fairtrade cannot be reduced to the label and its hopeful promise of 'a better deal' for producers. The label, or the product assurance it signifies, is underpinned by the Fairtrade standards and certification that give it meaning. These in turn are supported by Fairtrade governance structures. Accordingly, questions regarding multi-stakeholder participation need to be asked, to glean the level of ownership by different interest groups, including producers, of the process and the meaning of product assurance in Fairtrade. Likewise, an assessment of the relative compliance burdens imposed on stakeholders will allow some observations regarding the distribution of responsibilities that accompany Fairtrade product assurance, specifically analysing the burdens imposed on producers relative to traders.

This chapter traces the development and the mechanisms for Fairtrade product assurance, through the governance structure of Fairtrade labelling, with regard to the specific tasks of standard-setting and certification. First, following on from the discussion in the previous chapter, it clarifies the difference between the Fairtrade labelling model and the ATO model of Fair Trade. Second, it provides an examination of the relationship between governance and product assurance in Fairtrade labelling. Third, it evaluates the governance structures that support standard-setting and certification, with due attention to the engagement of different stakeholders (especially producers and traders), and accordingly the level of multi-stakeholder ownership of Fairtrade practices and priorities. Finally, it examines the key features of product assurance in Fairtrade, evaluating the applicability of generic and product-specific Fairtrade standards and compliance criteria to producers and traders, in turn focussing on the coffee case study.

In this chapter it is argued that the product assurance given in Fairtrade labelling signifies an ongoing multi-stakeholder participatory process, aiming to optimise the relevance and feasibility of standards and certification for participating producers and traders alike. Based on an analysis of Fairtrade policy documents outlining the procedures and rules that govern Fairtrade labelling, it is clear that there is an intention to ensure the participation of all internal stakeholders in the process of standard development and the guidance of certification procedures. However, while Fairtrade labelling has made vast improvements in the burdens it imposes on traders relative to producers, it continues to make demands on the business structure that producers adopt, a requirement that it fails in turn to demand of its traders. Indeed, this requirement has caused a major rift in the global Fairtrade system with its US operator – Fairtrade USA – opting to exit the system in late 2011. Finally, Fairtrade also fails to consult a broader spectrum of external stakeholders, such as Fairtrade consumers, who lack a direct voice in Fairtrade's governance structure.

Fairtrade and Fair Trade: Is there a difference?

Essentially, Fair Trade and Fairtrade share the same mandate, and are broadly committed to the same principles. In December 2001, four key international Fair Trade associations – FLO, IFAT, NEWS! and EFTA[2] (FINE) – representing labelling organisations and ATOs, arrived at a common definition of Fair Trade (Wills,[3] 2006, p. 10). This joint definition is still endorsed by both FLO (the international association for Fairtrade Labelling Organisations) and the WFTO (the international association for ATOs), who reinforced the definition almost word-for-word in a joint *Charter of Fair Trade Principles* published in January 2009 (WFTO and FLO International, 2009). Here, Fairtrade is defined as 'a trading partnership . . . that seeks greater equity in international trade . . . offering better trading conditions to, and securing the rights of marginalised producers and workers' (WFTO and FLO International, 2009). It also conceives of 'Fairtrade organisations, backed by consumers' as spanning producer support, awareness raising and campaigning activities (WFTO and FLO International, 2009).

The realisation of a common definition indicates the high level of unison in the objectives of Fairtrade-labelling organisations and ATOs. Marlike Kocken (2006, p. 5), on behalf of FINE, refers to 'two inseparable objectives' in Fair Trade (which clearly resound in the FINE definition of Fair Trade): to offer participating producers greater opportunities through Fair Trade arrangements, and to work towards better conditions for all producers through reform in the conventional market. In this respect both Fair Trade and Fairtrade seek to offer greater opportunities to producers within their own networks and to positively influence trading rules and practices in the conventional market. The difference in the application of Fair Trade principles, however, can be found in how these two models engage with the mainstream market. Indeed, Fairtrade labelling arose out of a desire to mainstream the Fair Trade concept beyond the confines of traditional ATO trading channels, which are typified by ATO-to-ATO trade. With the exception of the strategy of ATO product brands, such as Cafédirect, it is Fairtrade labelling that serves as the primary mainstream strategy developed within the Fair Trade movement.

The key premise of Fairtrade labelling is that Fairtrade products should be more easily accessible to consumers to achieve a growth in demand for Fair Trade products and thereby provide greater capacity for Fair Trade to assist marginalised producers in the developing world. While ATOs traditionally rely on their own reputation to guarantee their products as Fair Trade (today in some products, especially coffee, they also increasingly make use of the Fairtrade label), the concept of Fairtrade labelling provides this same guarantee for products distributed in conventional market spaces like supermarkets, bringing access to the highly prized consumers they serve. The device that makes this possible is the Fairtrade label itself. The key operational difference then, between the two Fair Trade models and the guarantees they provide, is that

- ATO Fair Trade provides a *business assurance*, and it is through the credibility and reputation of ATO businesses that their products are guaranteed

- while Fairtrade labelling provides a *product assurance* for any products that have the Fairtrade label, without making any claims about the businesses that trade or sell Fairtrade products

Accordingly, ATOs and Fairtrade labelling organisations are inherently different types of organisations. Tallontire (2002, p. 12) notes that the key difference between the two is that ATOs 'are active in trade themselves', while Fairtrade labelling organisations 'establish and monitor Fair Trade criteria, awarding labels to products that meet these standards'. It is through this ability to guarantee that products, rather than whole businesses, are Fair Trade, that Fairtrade labelling gains entry into the free market. An examination of the administrative structure of Fairtrade labelling underscores this point.

Administering Fairtrade: Bridging the free and the fair market

Together, the various arms of the FLO system undertake a range of functions that essentially set the parameters for trade that employs the Fairtrade label. They do not participate in the trade itself, but set the standards for the trade, ensure compliance to these standards, award the label, and promote both Fairtrade itself and the label specifically, as well as providing some measures of producer support. Fairtrade Labelling Organisations International[4] (FLO) is the umbrella organisation that presides over the Fairtrade system. It oversees both the functions of standard-setting and certification, which are necessary for the development and maintenance of a reputable label. However, where it once controversially was 'both the custodian and the certifier of the standards' (Ponte, 2004, p. 22), its administrative functions with regard to these tasks have changed considerably over time. Today, FLO serves as the international association for a membership of (National) Labelling Initiatives (LIs) which represent consumer markets, as well as regional producer networks, which represent producers across Latin America and the Caribbean, Asia and Oceania and Africa.[5] It has, however, outsourced the responsibility for standard-setting to a separate but internal body called FLO e.V.[6] In turn it has outsourced Fairtrade certification to an independent commercial company, FLO-Cert GmbH (hereafter FLO-Cert) since 2003 (Wills, 2006, p. 10). This separation of powers has been crucial in raising the legitimacy of the institution and in turn the label it produces. Even so, while FLO e.V and FLO-Cert work independently of each other, they both work under the same Board of Directors,[7] a linkage that likely supports the need for synergy between the standard-setting function of FLO e.V and the auditing capacity and integrity of FLO-Cert.

Accordingly, a company can participate in the Fairtrade labelling system if it

- abides by FLO e.V's standards for engagement with producers as applicable to the products they wish to buy
- satisfies FLO-Cert auditing of the management of its Fairtrade products and its engagement with producers
- has a LI that operates in the market in which it wishes to distribute Fairtrade products

From an administrative point of view, there is no limit to the types of companies – 'Fair Trade' or conventional – that can seek to engage in Fairtrade. Nonetheless, given the complexities of this administrative system and the controversial participation of conventional businesses, the integrity of the governance of the Fairtrade system becomes crucial if Fairtrade's product assurance is to hold any value in the market.

Product assurance: A 'product' of Fairtrade governance

Governance in Fairtrade plays a vital role in ensuring the effectiveness and integrity of Fairtrade standards and certification. In particular, the level of embedded multi-stakeholder representation and consultation in the governance of Fairtrade affects the extent to which product assurance can be perceived as a multi-stakeholder development. In FLO's (2009a, p. 11) most recent strategic review, the organisation recognised the importance of building the capacity of its regional producer networks to represent producers but also 'to take on more responsibilities within the system so that over time they are on a more equal footing with the Labelling Initiatives as members of Fairtrade'. Indeed, the issue of producer representation in Fairtrade is particularly pertinent when assessing the integrity of multi-stakeholder representation.

In its role as an international association for Fairtrade organisations, FLO is responsible for guiding and maintaining the direction of Fairtrade globally. Until 2007, full membership rights and responsibilities were not apportioned equally between consumer markets and producing interests. Traditionally FLO membership was composed exclusively of the LIs that represent individual consumer markets. It was only on 25 May 2007 that full membership status was officially extended to the three regional Fairtrade producer networks (FLO, 2007a). The decision was the result of a vote by the LIs, and reflects a shift to greater producer ownership of Fairtrade, and a greater representation of producer needs in Fairtrade. Peter Gaynor, Director of Fairtrade Mark Ireland stated, 'We think it is important that producers are now co-owners of FLO – we are working to improve their situation and need to know what their priorities are' (FLO, 2007a). This new voice, extended to producers as full members of FLO, has been accommodated by changes to governance within FLO. LIs and producer networks now have their own assemblies within which to discuss issues that are relevant to them specifically (FLO, 2007a). Producers are now directly represented in the Annual General Assembly, where all members are invited to take part in discussions and make decisions on common issues, including the election of the all-important Board of Directors – the central driver in FLOs' governance structure.

The Board of Directors is required to have 14 members in total (of which one will be elected as Chair of the Board), comprising five representatives from the LIs, four representatives from producer organisations (at least one drawn from each regional producer network), two representatives from certified traders, and three external independent experts (FLO, 2011a). Currently, however, there are only four representatives from LIs and three from producer organisations (FLO, 2011b). Considering the importance of producers to Fairtrade generally (indeed, to the very mission of Fairtrade) and the recent formal recognition of producers in FLO's membership, the number of Directors on the Board that represent producers appears to maintain an imbalance of power. This is particularly clear when one considers that by adding the two trader representatives to those for LIs, there are seven Board members representing the interests of Fairtrade consumption, compared to a possible four representing producers.[8] In addition, FLO's Leadership Team which manages the day-to-day running of the organisation, as well as matters of strategic direction (FLO, 2011a) currently has six members, none of which has a producer background and indeed two previously worked in senior capacities for national LIs (FLO, 2011c). In contrast, FLOs Standards Committee, discussed further, permits a greater representation of producers in its composition. Yet generally, there appears an uneven representation of internal stakeholders at the very top of FLOs governance structure. In addition, there is a dearth of formal representation from external stakeholders across the board.

While Fairtrade holds itself accountable to its internal stakeholders – these including producers, LIs and traders – it could be argued that it should also be held accountable to a range of external stakeholders. This is particularly the case if one conceives of FLO as a 'transnational organisation engaged in global governance', and wielding 'significant decision-making and norm-setting power' (van den Berghe, 2006, pp. 1, 2). Van den Berghe is critical of governance in the FLO system for a number of reasons, including internal stakeholder representation. For example, he faults the lack of representation of a broad spectrum of 'middlemen'. This is evident in the limited representation of traders in the Board of Directors. The limited voice afforded to 'traders' conflates the interests of 'processors, exporters, importers and manufacturers' (van den Berghe, 2006, p. 8). However, he is also critical of the lack of representation of external stakeholders. This includes consumers who are simply left with the 'all or nothing' recourse of buying or not buying Fairtrade products without the scope 'to make any meaningful, constructive and positive contribution to the formulation of standards' (van den Berghe, 2006, p. 7). Similarly, he argues that the many non-certified producers that are excluded from Fairtrade should be represented, particularly as the higher prices paid in the Fairtrade system run the risk of spurring overproduction of commodities and thereby could negatively impact prices in the conventional market which these producers supply (see van den Berghe, 2006, p. 8). While Fairtrade engages independent external experts for the composition of its Board of Directors and permits public scrutiny of key processes such as the development of Fairtrade standards (FLO Standards Unit, 2012a, p. 8), there is no formal recognition or allowance for the direct participation of key external stakeholders such as those flagged by van den Berghe. As such, the inward focus of Fairtrade's governance structure is limiting for a system which positions itself as a working 'fair' trade model. This is also apparent across its standard-setting and certification roles.

Standard-setting: Governance and engagement with stakeholders

Fairtrade standards are the foundation of product assurance in Fairtrade. It is these standards – comprising social, economic (including minimum prices as well as premiums), labour (that is, regarding labour conditions) and environmental standards – that set the terms and the parameters for the trading relationships sanctioned by Fairtrade. FLO e.V, under the guidance of an overseeing Standards Committee (SC), is the institutional arm that is responsible for developing and reviewing Fairtrade standards. This branch of the FLO system, through its staffing, its dedicated units and its structured consultations with stakeholders, is designed to ensure that Fairtrade standard-setting is a multi-stakeholder process, considering the priorities and requirements of the very interest groups that will bear the impact of Fairtrade standards. Certainly from a procedural point of view, multi-stakeholder representation has been achieved.

An examination of the composition of the SC is indicative of the strong culture of multi-stakeholder engagement for all standard-setting activities. Alike the Board of Directors itself, which is composed of a multi-stakeholder membership, the SC has a similarly representative demographic in its membership. As a separate institutional arm within the FLO umbrella, the SC was created by the Board of Directors and is responsible for guiding activities and making decisions pertaining to Fairtrade standards, which are then executed by the Fairtrade Standards Unit (SU, see discussion further) (FLO Standards Unit, 2012a, p. 4). The Terms of Reference (TOR) for the FLO Standards Committee clarifies FLOs current approach to the composition of the SC. The SC must have an uneven composition of a minimum of five and a maximum of 11 members, though currently it comprises an even six members in total (FLO, 2011d, p. 2). There must be a balance in the representation of suppliers (here FLO differentiates producers from workers) and users in addition to any nominated independent experts (FLO, 2011d, p. 2). Unlike the Board of Directors which provides for greater representation of LIs than producer organisations, producers currently have a greater representation in the SC. At present it comprises one representative from the LIs, three from the producer organisations (one each from Asia, Latin America and Africa), one representative for traders and one representative for a Fairtrade Trader Organisation (an ATO as per previous chapter) (FLO, 2012a). Producers certainly have greater representation in the SC, which alike the Board of Directors, also features inclusive representation of producers from all producing regions. Multi-stakeholder representation is also clearly valued in standard-setting processes.

The development of Fairtrade standards in FLO e.V, draws on a number of devices through which multi-stakeholder input is sought. These include structured consultation with stakeholders, an important part of the procedures for setting and reviewing Fairtrade standards. The stakeholders consulted, run the gamut of those involved in the marketing chain of a product, as well as units within FLO, FLO-Cert and the LI's (FLO Standards Unit, 2012b, p. 1). The role of the different units within FLO e.V, and how they engage stakeholders in the production and trade of a product, are outlined in the 'Standard Operating Procedures: Development of Fairtrade Standards'; the 'Standard Operating Procedures: Development of Fairtrade Minimum Prices and Premiums' and the 'Standard Operating Procedures: Complaints against Fairtrade Standards Setting' (FLO Standards Unit, 2012a, 2012c and 2012d). While these documents do not show the level of response from different interests groups (e.g. producers compared to traders) or the relative authority of their recommendations on the final decisions made by FLO e.v, they do show that there is considerable consultation with stakeholders, which is structured into the schedule of standard-setting procedures, and that stakeholders are involved in the final decision-making.

Stakeholders can make a proposal for developing a new standard or reviewing an existing standard. The SU, which is sub-divided into a Pricing Subunit (PSU) and Standards Subunit (SSU), manages Fairtrade standard-setting and deals with such requests (FLO Standards Unit, 2012a, p. 3). Stakeholders can make a formal request to either change an existing standard or create a new standard (FLO Standards Unit, 2012a, p. 4), and they can also lodge a 'procedural complaint' to contest the way that a standard was developed (FLO Standards Unit, 2012a, p. 3). Once a request to develop a standard has been accepted, the SU is responsible for developing a plan and works with the Producer Services and Relations Unit (PSRU), FLO-Cert and the LIs to canvas the needs of stakeholders (FLO Standards Unit, 2012a, p. 6). Indeed, the input of a broad range of stakeholders is targeted through the 'research' and 'consultation' phases (FLO Standards Unit, 2012a, pp. 7–8), which form a crucial part of the standard-setting process. Finally, as the SC approves any major new standards or revisions (FLO Standards Unit, 2012a, p. 9),[9] stakeholder input comes into play through representatives serving on the SC. The creation of multiple avenues for engaging stakeholders in standard-setting shows a commitment to providing a range of opportunities for stakeholders to influence the development of standards. Notably, producers are provided with an opportunity to raise concerns about Fairtrade standards and any associated minimum prices and premiums through their own formal regional networks, as well as dedicated producer support unit.

A crucial element of FLOs administrative capacity is its producer support service. The inclusion of a dedicated PSRU is indicative of the relatively recent recognition in the FLO governance structure of the importance of ensuring that standards complement the needs and priorities of producers in particular. FLO established the PSRU (formally Producer Business Unit) in 2004 to provide support and advice to producers (FLO, 2009b). In addition, the PSRU provides producers with an important platform from which they can present their interests. Table 5.1 deconstructs the scope of the PSRU, highlighting its presence in producing countries and its producer support roles. The PSRU undertakes its responsibilities as a producer dedicated unit, through direct access to producers as facilitated by its extensive presence in producing

Table 5.1 FLOs PSRU: Scope of support for Fairtrade producers

Date established	2004
Purpose	Producer support through
	• training
	• advice on certification
	• assisting relationships with buyers and accessing new markets
	• assisting producer engagement in the consultation process for standards and pricing
	• aiding producer efforts to network and develop partnerships
Presence in producing countries	Ten regional coordinators typically based in producing regions (these support the work of three regional heads based in FLO headquarters in Germany)
	Liaison officers providing support across more than 50 countries[a]
Support roles	Includes providing information, training and advice to producers
Role regarding Fairtrade standards	Request development of new/revision of existing Fairtrade standards, minimum prices and premiums
	May be enlisted by the PSU to serve as 'project manager' for a price request (regarding Fairtrade prices and/or premiums), overseeing research and consultation with key stakeholders such as producers

Note:
[a] High growth in coverage from only 16 countries as at August 2006 (FLO, 2006a).
Sources: FLO (2011e, 2011f); FLO Standards Unit (2012a and 2012c).

countries and regions. In particular, the PSRUs liaison officers provide a support role to producers, including the provision of information, training and advice (FLO, 2011e). However, the PSRU pipeline to producers works both ways, with the PSRU not only responsible for providing information and support, but also receiving and managing particular producer inputs and requests, as well as those of other stakeholders.

The PSRU also plays an important role in the process of standard-setting, especially with regard to issues that are particularly important for producers. The minimum price is developed to adequately represent 'average costs of sustainable production' (FLO Standards Unit, 2012c, p. 4) and both minimum prices and premiums may be set at a global, regional or national level (FLO, 2012b, p.2). As such, in the research stage, input from producers is sought, often with the assistance of the PSRU and its liaison officers based in producing countries (see FLO Standards Unit,

2012c, pp.8–9 and FLO Standards Unit, 2010, p. 3). However, input to the PSRU is not limited to producers alone and, equally, producers can convey their concerns through other divisions within FLO as well as their own Producer Networks. Indeed, another which producers will deal with regularly is FLO's certification body, FLO-Cert.

Certification: Governance and engagement with stakeholders

Certification is as fundamental to product assurance in Fairtrade as are the Fairtrade standards themselves. Among its goals, FLO's certification arm – FLO-Cert – includes the aspiration '[t]o provide a guarantee to consumers that Fairtrade Standards are rigorously controlled, thereby bringing credibility and sustainability to the Fairtrade market' (FLO-Cert, 2012a). Certification ensures that standards are met and maintained by all participants in Fairtrade and therefore apply to Fairtrade products. The integrity of certification procedures and the extent to which these are appropriate and relevant, impacts the effectiveness of Fairtrade certification as a viable mechanism for ensuring Fairtrade standards are complied with. While the internal structure of FLO-Cert mirrors many aspects of that of FLO e.V, its engagement with stakeholders is quite different, arguably because the burden of standard-setting as compared to conducting certifications entails a greater necessity for stakeholder involvement.

As with FLO standards, it is clear that a higher level of multi-stakeholder participation results in a higher level of multi-stakeholder ownership of certification procedures. However, the necessity for multi-stakeholder involvement in FLO-Cert is less pressing as this organisation is not responsible for making the rules and is rather cast in the role of rule 'enforcer'. Indeed, the criteria against which producers and traders are certified by FLO-Cert, are contained in the standards produced by FLO e.V. The central issues of stakeholder input relates to the practicality and integrity of compliance criteria necessary for certification. These are dealt with through the various avenues available in FLO e.V, where changes to the standard are proposed and executed. FLO-Cert itself may also submit a request for a new or revised standard (FLO Standards Unit, 2012a, p. 4). However, within the organisational structure of FLO-Cert, there are a number of levels of organisation that directly engage stakeholders, allowing for further opportunities for stakeholder input and influence in certification.

FLO-Cert, while maintaining that it 'operates as a completely autonomous and separate organisation' is indeed 'fully owned by FLO e.V and shares the same vision' (FLO-Cert, 2007a). Yet a shared Board of

Directors (FLO, 2007b, p. 6) maintains oversight over both organisations. At the head of its own internal structure, FLO-Cert is guided by its own Supervisory Board and then its CEO (FLO-Cert, 2012b). In 2007, FLO-Cert explained the composition of its then Advisory Board to 'comprise[s] a balance of key stakeholders such as certified operators, independent certification experts and consumer representation' (FLO-Cert, 2007a). Concern for producer representation is not evident in this statement and, rather, FLO-Cert's role in providing product assurance in consumer markets is underscored. FLO-Cert may appear as an institution that by design is working at arm's length from producers, likely a necessary attribute to maintain independence in its role as certifier. Even so, it works directly with producers on the ground through its auditing activities, which in turn ensures that this organisation has a great impact on the producers' experience of Fairtrade. In this respect, FLO-Cert is well positioned to engage with producers with offices in India, Costa Rica and South Africa, as well as over 100 auditors working across 50 countries in the South (FLO-Cert, 2012c).

The issue of governance and in particular, multi-stakeholder engagement are key to evaluating the relevance of the FLO regulatory system to producers. Broadly, efforts at multi-stakeholder engagement are clearly entrenched in FLOs institutional culture, although internal stakeholder participation is prioritised over that of external stakeholders. However, the key test of the organisations relevance to producers lies in an analysis of the Fairtrade standards it has developed, which participating producers must abide.

Fairtrade standards: Rights and responsibilities of traders and producers

The process by which standards and certification are developed and administered in Fairtrade – insofar as it represents and engages stakeholders in both the production and trade of a product – is integral to the legitimacy of a system that is designed not only to be viable but also to represent and serve the needs of a targeted interest group. As the following two chapters will evaluate the impact of Fairtrade labelling on smallholder coffee producers – coffee is the most established Fairtrade-labelled product, and to a large degree offers the best opportunity to evaluate the effectiveness of Fairtrade labelling – the key focus in this section will be on Fairtrade standards applicable to coffee. While it is clear that producers generally are engaged in developing standards and have some involvement in the governance of certification, the crucial test to how well Fairtrade represents producers – herein specifically smallholder coffee producers – lies in a second level of analysis, assessing the scope of the standards themselves and the burden of their application.

In any Fairtrade product there are generic standards that apply, as well as product-specific standards, which are designed to address the particular economic and social requirements in the production and trade of a unique product range. This section assesses the scope of generic and product-specific standards with regard to their applicability to traders and also to two distinct types of producers: smallholder producers (hereinafter producers and small/small-scale/smallholder producers will be used interchangeably) and hired labour, particularly focusing on the smallholder producers and the traders of Fairtrade coffee. The implications of Fairtrade standards, regarding the relative responsibilities conferred on traders and producers, will be considered. Finally, the recently created Generic Trade Standard, which only came into force in February 2009, will be examined. This will show that the introduction of a trade standard, while an important step in addressing the uneven treatment of producers and traders in the history of Fairtrade, still makes limited demands of traders participating in Fairtrade, relative to the demands made of participating producers.

Fairtrade labelling: Scope of the standards

Generic standards are essentially the first point of reference for producers and traders that wish to participate in Fairtrade. Currently there are two types of generic standards: generic producer standards and generic trade standards. Generic standards for Fairtrade production further differentiate between two forms of labour mobilisation: small-scale producers and hired labour. Accordingly, there are standards for small-scale producers (organised into democratic organisational structures),[10] and hired labour (specifying, for example, the right for workers to join trade unions) (FLO, 2011h). Producers and traders need to first establish whether there are Fairtrade standards for a desired product, and what types of labour mobilisation are certified for a desired product. For traders, this is as simple as ensuring that there is a Fairtrade product standard for the product they wish to trade, and ensuring that they make the appropriate choice of trading with either smallholder organisations or hired labour (in some cases, both types of producer partners are allowed for a product category) to qualify for Fairtrade certification. Producers must also establish that there are Fairtrade standards for their product, but they must further check to see whether the product standard only applies to either small farmers' organisations or hired labour, or if it applies to both. The absence of provision for both smallholder producers' organisations and hired labour in some product categories typically reflects differences in how products are produced. For example, smallholder producers predominantly produce coffee and cocoa and products like tea are typically grown in hired labour situations.

Currently there are only six product categories that provide for the participation of hired labour, with production in flowers and plants and sports balls exclusively dedicated to hired-labour production (see Table 5.2). With the exception of these two categories, small producers' organisations may participate in all of the remaining product categories. In the case of coffee, current standards only provide for the certification of small farmers' organisations, without provision for hired-labour production of coffee to date.[11] Specific requirements for coffee are contained in the Fairtrade Standard for Coffee for Small Producer Organisations (hereinafter Coffee Standard); however, as directed in this document, smallholder producers must first consult the applicable generic standards documents (FLO, 2011i, p. 3). Accordingly, producer organisations must also consult the Fairtrade Standard for Small Producer Organisations (hereinafter Producer Standard) and the Generic Fairtrade Trade Standard (hereinafter Trade Standard) (FLO, 2011j, 2011k). In conjunction with

Table 5.2 Fairtrade product standards for small farmers and hired labour

Labour type	Small farmers	Hired labour	Both
Product category	Cane sugar	Flowers and	Fresh fruit
	Cereals	plants	Prepared and
	Cocoa	Sports balls	preserved fruit
	Coffee		Fresh vegetables
	Fibre crops		Secondary
	Gold		products
	Herbs, herbal teas		
	and spices		
	Honey		
	Nuts		
	Oilseeds and		
	oleaginous fruit		
	Prepared and		
	preserved fruit		
	and vegetables		
	Tea		
	Timber		
	Pulses and potatoes		

Sources: FLO (2011l, 2011m).

any specifications in the Coffee Standard, these set out the rules of engagement for Fairtrade coffee producers and traders.[12]

Fairtrade standards: Key criteria for producers

The Fairtrade Producer Standard (FLO, 2011j) is a comprehensive document outlining relevant Fairtrade standards and compliance criteria. The standards contained in this document are supported by accompanying criteria where: core requirements set out mandatory requirements synonymous with key Fairtrade principles; and development requirements set out benchmarks for ongoing improvement, which producer organisations must achieve over time by meeting 'minimum average thresholds' (FLO, 2011j, p. 5). Core requirements are necessary to ensure that the promises and (product) assurances made by Fairtrade are upheld in practice. Formerly referred to as 'minimum requirements', they are intended to ensure the integrity of Fairtrade, so that benefits reach producers, and overall that 'standards . . . fundamental to ensuring the rights of the members and workers of the producer organisation, as well as those of buyers and consumers' are protected (FLO, 2010a, p. 4). Development requirements, while also essential, are more flexible as they can be realised after certification.

The Producer Standard, like all Fairtrade Standard documents, is organised into four chapters comprising: General Requirements (explaining Fairtrade criteria for the structure and membership of producer organisations); Trade (including specification, for example, regarding contracts and the use of the Fairtrade mark); Production (including management practices at an organisational level, and criteria for the protection of the environment and labour rights); and, finally, Business and Development specifications (which cover measures for producer empowerment and development) (FLO, 2011j). The standards related to environmental protection, which may, for example, contribute to the health of smallholder producers, largely stand on their own merit, and are not singularly driven towards the welfare of smallholder producers and their communities. Meanwhile, standards related to labour conditions, outlining criteria for key issues like discrimination and child labour rights, are more or less relevant for different smallholder organisations, depending on their use (if any) of hired labour. For crops like coffee, which are less labour intensive than, for example, those for fresh fruit or vegetables, there is less reliance on hired labour (FLO, 2011j, p. 7). Of particular interest in assessing the potential benefits of Fairtrade for smallholder coffee producers then, are the standards with regard to the collective organisation of producers, as well as those pertaining to trade and to business and development.

Fairtrade requires that smallholder producers be organised and that at least half of the membership of such producer organisations are smallholders, who in turn must produce at least half of the volume of product sold as Fairtrade (FLO, 2011j, p. 7). This is likely one of the more controversial features of Fairtrade. It clearly targets organised producers, stating in the Producer Standard that it aims to 'ensure that the direct beneficiaries of Fairtrade are small producers, including their families who are organised into producer organisations' (FLO, 2011j, p. 28). In addition, Fairtrade arguably micromanages the structure of these organisations through its rules on issues such as 'participation' and 'transparency', and by stipulating that they 'should have democratic structures in place' (see FLO, 2011j, p. 30). This requirement is perhaps one of the strongest features of Fairtrade, as by pooling their resources smallholder producers can work to strengthen their position vis-à-vis other actors in the global trade even without gaining Fairtrade certification (see discussion in Chapter 7). Yet it also works to exclude a large number of producers from access to Fairtrade markets. This is a key reason that TransFair USA, which has since adopted the new name 'Fair Trade USA' (FTUSA), chose to exit the Fairtrade system.

In a joint statement, Fair Trade USA and FLO (2011) announced that 'Fair Trade USA has decided to resign its membership of the Fairtrade International (FLO) system effective December 31, 2011'. In an article authored by FTUSA's CEO, Paul Rice (2012), he argues that the organisation 'has chosen to buck the status quo . . . to make Fair Trade truly fair for all'. Starting with coffee, the organisation plans to 'adapt Fair Trade standards for both workers on large farms and independent small farmers', to establish a 'more inclusive model', which will cater to the over four million farmers it estimates have been excluded from Fairtrade markets (Rice, 2012). This criticism does point to the limitations of Fairtrade, as it only caters to a niche of well-organised producers (see discussion in Chapter 6). Alternatively, FTUSA's move could be seen to water down the very integrity of the Fairtrade model, by pitting small-producing interests against much bigger plantations. Certainly the regional producer networks that supply Fairtrade have all voiced their concern about the action FTUSA has taken and FLO has also questioned the move with regard to coffee in particular, which it claims has a typically transient workforce, which poses difficulties for ensuring that Fairtrade benefits reach them (FLO, 2011n).

In addition to criteria set out in the Producer Standard, coffee producers must look to the Coffee Standard. This document is intended to supplement those standards already drafted in the Producer and Trader

Standard documents with any product-specific criteria. Accordingly, in some cases no additional criteria are set out. For example, in chapter two concerned with 'Trade', no additional requirements are provided for the standards relating to traceability or product composition. In turn, chapter three on 'Production' has no additional criteria for any standards.

The main additions to the generic standards relate to trade and business development (the latter also relating to trade) discussed further, as well as the scope of coffee production and trade. Specifically, Fairtrade in coffee makes provision for trade in the two coffee varieties that currently dominate the conventional coffee market – Arabica and Robusta – and applies to a variety of processing systems (FLO, 2011i, p. 4).[13] It also makes provision for the purchase and sale of coffee in green bean form (FLO, 2011i, p. 4).[14] To further examine Fairtrade's trade standards, it is important to also examine the generic standards that apply.

Trade standards: Implications for traders and producers

Until recently, there was a glaring gap in Fairtrade rules with the absence of a generic standard for traders, especially considering that the generic Producer Standard is much more detailed in terms of compliance criteria than those outlined for traders in the Coffee Standard. This had implications for the burden of compliance for producers relative to traders. On 16 February 2009 Generic Fairtrade Trade Standards (FLO, 2009d, p. 4) came into effect to address this oversight. Like the Generic Standards for smallholder producers, these must be read in conjunction with the relevant product standards – here coffee – complementing the provisions contained therein. However, in many ways the Generic Trade Standard is broader in scope than the existing Generic Standards for producers (i.e. smallholder producers and hired labour), containing standards that are relevant to the spectrum of participants in production through to trade of a Fairtrade product.

The Trade Standard outlines the scope of applicability for traders, defining the types of traders that are subject to compliance. It stipulates that '[e]very operator buying or selling certified products, up to the point where the certified product is in its final packaging for the consumer' is subject to comply (FLO, 2011k, p. 3). Like producers, traders are subject to certification, although the language regarding audits is much stronger for producers. Producers are advised: '[Y]ou must accept audits of your premises and subcontracted premises and provide information at the certification body's request (FLO, 2011j, p. 7). In contrast, traders are advised: 'Operators will be subject to an audit process determined by the certification body to assess their compliance with this Standard' (FLO, 2011k, p. 5). The key difference in requirements is apparent when you consider that the Trade Standard is not divided into mandatory (i.e. 'core') and progress (i.e. 'development') criteria. While there are careful explanations of criteria in the Trade Standard, they are not clear and measurable to the same degree as those supporting the Producer Standard.

Table 5.3 Fairtrade trade standard (for coffee)

Standards:	Scope of selected compliance criteria
Traceability	Aims to ensure that operators only sell Fairtrade products as Fairtrade by ensuring that the authenticity of Fairtrade products is verifiable
Product composition	Specifies that food composite products contain a minimum of 20% Fairtrade-certified products with the aim to include as high a percentage of these as possible
Contracts	Includes the following provisions: • Buyers are obliged to sign purchase contracts with producers, which at a minimum must include specifications on volume, price, payment terms, delivery conditions and quality • Buyers and sellers may, by agreement, fix prices for product exchanged on a future delivery date
Sustaining trade	Aims to foster a sustainable trade relationship through which producer capacity is nurtured through a number of devices, including information sharing, provision of sourcing plans to producers (enabling producers to plan production taking into consideration matters like delivery dates), providing additional assistance like training and price updates where possible Buyers are prohibited from making the purchase of Fairtrade-certified products a condition of purchase of non-certified products where the terms of the latter are disadvantageous for producers
Pre-finance	Buyers are obliged to provide up to 60% of the contract value in the form of pre-finance. Interest may be charged but cannot be above the buyer's current borrowing costs
Pricing	Stipulates that buyers must pay the Fairtrade minimum price (or market price if this is higher) as well as a Fairtrade premium, where this applies to a Fairtrade product. Standards include criteria to ensure prompt and transparent payments to producers The Coffee Standard also stipulates that producers must invest a minimum of US$0.05 cents/lb of the Fairtrade Premium into productivity and/or quality improvements

Sources: FLO, 2011i, 2011k.

As trade describes a two-way exchange, it is interesting to look at criteria for trade across both the Coffee Standard and the Trade Standard, with reflection on their implications for traders and producers in turn. Criteria relevant to the coffee trade are primarily contained in chapters two and four of both Standards, specifically chapter two on Trade and chapter four on Business and Development. Table 5.3 outlines the key standards that apply as well as the scope of the key associated compliance criteria. It is primarily drawn from the Trade Standard, which is more comprehensive on this matter.

Conclusion

Fairtrade relies on the device of a label to provide an assurance to consumers that its products are produced and traded according to Fairtrade principles. However, the real meaning of the label rests with the Fairtrade standards and compliance criteria, which have been developed to support Fairtrade principles and which must be enforced if the label is to hold any integrity. This chapter has examined the governance structures that support Fairtrade labelling, focussing on the process and outcomes of standard-setting and certification development. Analysis has been especially focused on the participation of stakeholders, in particular, the representation of smallholder producers in Fairtrade governance structures and in the standards and compliance criteria relevant to coffee. As Fairtrade seeks to benefit its member producers, it is important that governance structures and processes with regard to standard-setting and certification, as well as the substance of the standards themselves, also represent the particular needs of producers. Certainly there are a number of opportunities for producers to participate in Fairtrade governance, but the real significance of producers' participation is not clear. When examining the relative burdens of certification, as imposed on traders compared to smallholder producers' organisations, it is clear that Fairtrade has made significant improvements to its standards and accompanying verification systems. Yet, as will be shown in Chapter 6, the standards imposed on producers require a structural model for organisation that maintains a high barrier of entry for producers relative to traders. Indeed, this has fuelled the call by a number of ATOs to look closely at the treatment of conventional businesses in Fairtrade to ensure commensurate demands are made of their business structures (see Chapter 8). A further evaluation of the challenge of complying with Fairtrade standards for smallholder producers' organisations will be advanced in the following chapter.

6
Fairtrade Coffee: A Niche Market

Fairtrade proposes to be an open system, which especially targets marginalised producers, yet there are a number of factors that determine eligibility. In order to undertake an evaluation of Fairtrade's impact on marginalised producers, it is first necessary to clearly understand the scope of Fairtrade markets, including the rules and trends that determine producer capacity to participate. An understanding of the terms of access, which characterise entry into Fairtrade labelling, provides insights into how viable an alternative the Fairtrade labelling model is for producers on a whole, or whether this is a system that works only for a privileged minority.

This analysis, which focuses on the coffee case study, is developed in two ways. First, by identifying trends in Fairtrade production, noting the patterns of inclusion and exclusion regionally. Second, by examining key factors that may help to explain these trends, such as the rules and procedures that govern access to Fairtrade markets (following on from the discussion in the previous chapter). There are significant geographic trends with respect to grower participation in Fairtrade labelling, and the potential to increase producer participation globally largely requires growing the capacity of Fairtrade markets, first and foremost. In addition, the administrative requirements and the costs for producers to participate in Fairtrade, affects producer access to Fairtrade markets and accordingly, it leaves the most marginalised producers disenfranchised. In the case of coffee, producer access is determined on the basis of factors such as organisational structure, financial capacity, resources and skills. Finally, Fairtrade standards and accompanying compliance criteria dictate a number of producer capacities, which affect eligibility to successfully apply for Fairtrade certification. Essentially, the terms of access in this analysis refers to some of the prerequisite capacities, resources and organisational features that producers will need to be eligible to participate in Fairtrade labelling.

An examination of producer access to Fairtrade coffee markets in particular, indicates that the rules and conditions of access to these markets are designed for a specific profile of producer organisation. These producer groups need to

- be well-resourced in terms of start-up financial capital (self-funded or sourced)
- be equipped with basic administrative resources (including basic communications infrastructure) and skills
- operate as organisational structures that are democratically controlled by a majority smallholder membership
- manage the scale of operations and levels of bureaucracy in their organisations
- source a demand for their Fairtrade products in often limited Fairtrade markets.

Individual smallholder coffee producers will not gain access to Fairtrade markets unless they first manage to organise in this way and have the resources and skills to successfully meet all the standards and criteria necessary to achieve Fairtrade certification. While Fairtrade labelling aims to reach the most marginalised producers, this goal cannot be realised when the barriers to entering Fairtrade remain so high. The problem of grower capacities illustrates that Fairtrade is a niche market solution with limited capacity to draw smallholder coffee producers into its ranks. It is therefore constrained in the opportunities it offers the majority of smallholder coffee producers, which continue to supply the conventional commercial market.

Fairtrade markets: Trends in producer access

The growth that Fairtrade labelling has experienced in just over 20 years has been phenomenal. Its starting point in 1988 was one product (coffee), one market (the Netherlands) and one origin (Mexico). However, a coffee monopoly in Fairtrade labelling only lasted for approximately five years, ending in 1993 when cocoa/chocolate certification was introduced, quickly followed by tea certification in 1994, and banana certification in 1996 (Eshuis and Harmsen, 2003, p. 9). Today, there are 20 product lines (FLO, 2011l, 2011m). Almost three-quarters of all Fairtrade sales income in 2009–10 was provided by just three of these product lines: coffee

(44.7 per cent), bananas (19.1 per cent) and cocoa (11.1 per cent) (FLO, 2011o, p. 47). Nonetheless, with an ever-expanding range of Fairtrade products, opportunities for producers in Fairtrade markets are clearly expanding. Indeed, by 2007 seven per cent of coffee producers also produced one or more additional Fairtrade products (FLO, 2007c). The underlying significance of this expansion, however, is that the Fairtrade model has extended beyond its original dependency on coffee, although it still dominates as the leading source of sales income. Yet which producers participate is not just a question of available Fairtrade product lines.

Geographic trends in production and constraints in consumer market capacity are two important interrelated factors, which largely explain the dynamics of producer inclusion and exclusion in the Fairtrade supplier base. Clear geographic trends in Fairtrade production illustrate the relative competitiveness of different producing regions. Additionally, Fairtrade's market capacity, with consequences for its viable production levels, continues to inhibit the ability to reach marginalised producers who could arguably benefit from participation in Fairtrade. In fact, limitations in the Fairtrade market already impact the ability for Fairtrade labelling to cater to its existing producers, let alone new producers. As such it is unlikely that entrenched geographic patterns of production will shift significantly, or that the hope to reach the most marginalised producers can be fulfilled.

Regional representation in Fairtrade production

Growth in Fairtrade across all products has been unevenly spread across producing regions, and has been least satisfactory with regard to Asian origins. In 2010 at least 1.1 million producers participated in Fairtrade, comprising 938,000 farmers and 163,000 workers (FLO, 2011o, p. 17).[1] There is a clear dominance of origins from Latin America and the Caribbean (hereinafter Latin America) in terms of the number of producer organisations participating in Fairtrade. This leadership is clearly tipped on its head, however, when examining the data of individual producers representation.

Figure 6.1 indicates that as a percentage of total producers' organisations supplying Fairtrade in 2010, Latin American origins represented 56.2 per cent, African origins 27.9 per cent, and origins from Asia and Oceania (hereinafter Asia) 15.8 per cent. In contrast, as a percentage of individual producers, African origins account for 58.1 per cent, Latin American origins account for 25.8 per cent and Asian origins remained steady (in comparison to percentages by organisation) at 15.9 per cent of total producers. However, as also indicated in Figure 6.1, Latin American

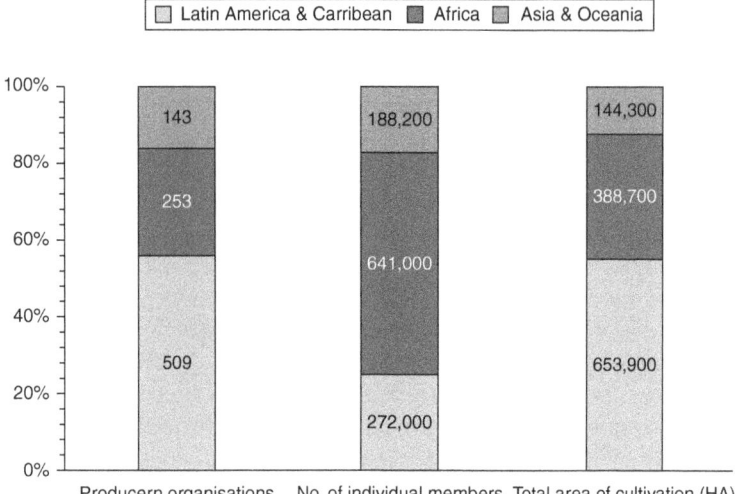

Figure 6.1 Fairtrade producers across regions (2010)
Source: FLO (2011o, pp. 19, 29, 42).

origins cultivate more land across the board,[2] explaining and restoring the dominance of this region in Fairtrade production by the measure of Fairtrade incomes.

Figure 6.2 assesses regional representation in Fairtrade production by another measure: Fairtrade income (sales revenues and premium payments). This shows that for 2009–10, Latin America accounted for 69.4 per cent of Fairtrade sales revenue, with Africa only accounting for 24.4 per cent and Asia a mere 6.1 per cent. Pérez Sueiro (2006, p. 55) attributes the Latin American dominance in the production of 'Fairtrade food products' to 'historical reasons within the Fairtrade movement'. Certainly Fairtrade coffee, and thus the Fairtrade model, was pioneered by the first Fairtrade initiative in the Netherlands (Max Havelaar) at the request of a Latin American producer group (Fairtrade Foundation, 2006). In fact, coffee continues to dominate Fairtrade production. This becomes clear when we consider sales revenue data for coffee in 2009–10 (€ 242,772,000) as well as premium money received (€ 17,491,000) (FLO, 2011o, p. 58). Accordingly, in percentage terms, coffee accounted for 44.1 per cent of sales revenue and 33.9 per cent of all premium money received in 2009–10. Thus, the Latin American dominance of Fairtrade production is largely explained by the ongoing dominance of this region in coffee production.

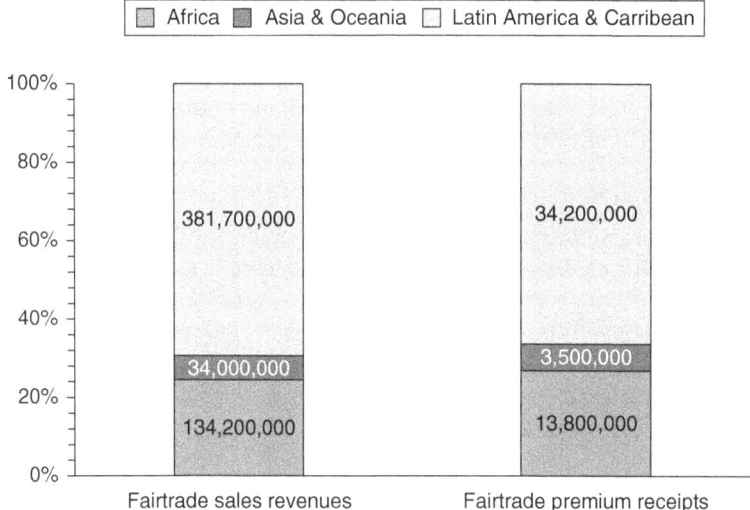

Figure 6.2   Fairtrade sales revenue and premium receipts (2009–10)
Source: FLO (2011o, pp. 71, 75, 79.

If we break the previous data down further, it becomes very clear that coffee largely accounts for Fairtrade's regional production trends. In 2009–10 329 producer organisations supplied Fairtrade coffee, representing 36 per cent of all Fairtrade producer organisations (FLO, 2011o, p. 56). 532,000 individual producers (FLO, 2011o, p. 57) highlight that coffee clearly dominates Fairtrade production, accounting for 50.6 per cent of all individual Fairtrade producers in 2009–10. Regional representation again mimicked trends for all Fairtrade products, with African origins accounting for 55.2 per cent of individual producers (293,700 producers); Latin America for 36.1 per cent (191,900 producers) and Asia for 8.7 per cent (46,300 producers) (see FLO, 2011o, p. 57). Coffee producers from Latin America once again dominated the category of area of land under cultivation with average plots of 2.4 hectares dwarfing their counterparts in Africa and Asia who cultivate plots averaging less than one hectare (FLO, 2011o, p. 46). Not surprisingly over 80 per cent of Fairtrade coffee was grown by producers in Latin America (FLO, 2011o, p. 56).

Production of Fairtrade coffee accounts for the largest slice of the 'Fairtrade production pie'. Looking closely at geographic trends within Fairtrade coffee production and across Fairtrade production generally, Africa and Asia are sidelined compared to the high participation of

Latin American origins, and Asian origins are in fact marginalised with particularly low participation rates. These trends are unlikely to change while market capacity (in terms of the ability of the Fairtrade market to absorb more producers) remains limited and constrained to a small niche of the conventional market.

The problem of market capacity

Despite the vision that Fairtrade labelling should serve as a mainstream strategy with access to a broader consumer base, it is nonetheless constrained with respect to the level of consumer interest it is able to generate in the conventional market. This has clear implications for producer access to Fairtrade markets in lieu of conventional commercial markets. In fact, with regard to market growth, Fairtrade coffee presents something of a contradiction. Figure 6.3 shows that since entry into its first market in the Netherlands in 1988, another 23 Fairtrade markets have

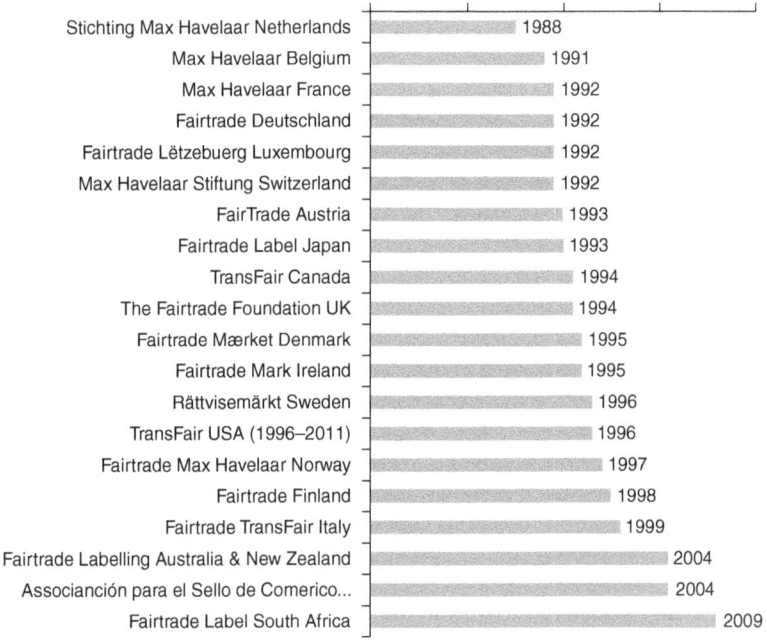

Stichting Max Havelaar Netherlands	1988
Max Havelaar Belgium	1991
Max Havelaar France	1992
Fairtrade Deutschland	1992
Fairtrade Lëtzebuerg Luxembourg	1992
Max Havelaar Stiftung Switzerland	1992
FairTrade Austria	1993
Fairtrade Label Japan	1993
TransFair Canada	1994
The Fairtrade Foundation UK	1994
Fairtrade Mærket Denmark	1995
Fairtrade Mark Ireland	1995
Rättvisemärkt Sweden	1996
TransFair USA (1996–2011)	1996
Fairtrade Max Havelaar Norway	1997
Fairtrade Finland	1998
Fairtrade TransFair Italy	1999
Fairtrade Labelling Australia & New Zealand	2004
Associancion para el Sello de Comerico...	2004
Fairtrade Label South Africa	2009

Figure 6.3   Fairtrade labelling: Evolution of markets[a]
Note:
[a] Fairtrade Labelling Australia and New Zealand covers two consumer markets and Fairtrade Finland covers four: Finland, Estonia, Lithuania and Latvia.
Sources: Linton, Liou and Shaw (2004, p. 229); FLO (2005, p. 18; 2011n; 2011o).

come on board. A notable blotch on this record is the recent exit of the US certifier, Fair Trade USA (formerly TransFair USA under the FLO system). However, this does not mean the US market has been excised from the FLO system, as currently TransFair Canada will oversee this market (see FLO, 2011n). Setting aside this recent controversy, growth rates in individual markets have been impressive, though the market share in individual consumer markets remains limited in terms of reaching a broader base of marginalised producers.

Table 6.1 shows that average annual growth in coffee sales volumes in many of the established markets has been very high, including over 8000 per cent for the US and high increases also in Spain, Canada, Finland, France, Japan and the United Kingdom; some of the older markets like Germany and Switzerland have tapered with minimal growth and the Netherlands has even experienced negative growth (this may also relate to an already high volume in the Netherlands compared to market size). This data shows that there has been a sustained

Table 6.1   Fairtrade coffee sales volume growth: 1999 and 2008[a] (MT)

Country	1999	2008	Average annual % growth
Austria	283.8	1000	+ 28
Australia/New Zealand	99 (2005)	299 (2006)	+ 202
Belgium	477.2	1218	+ 17
Canada	77.6	5037	+ 710
Denmark	695.4	733 (2006)	+ 1
Finland	35.6	800	+ 239
France	270.3	6630 (2007)	+ 294
Germany	3332.2	4962	+ 5
Ireland	40.5	500	+ 126
Italy	353.3	323 (2007)	– 1
Japan	6.2	147 (2006)	+ 324
Luxembourg	69.3	130	+ 10
Netherlands	3185.5	3100	– 0
Norway	54.7	751	+ 141
Spain	13 (2005)	347	+ 856
Sweden	218.2	3070	+ 145
Switzerland	1429	1530 (2007)	+ 1
United Kingdom	1237.1	34,383	+ 298
US	55	39,813	+ 8032

Note:
[a] Data is generally 1999–2008, variations are marked in the table.
Sources: FLO (2006b; 1999 and 2006 data); FAO (2009, pp. 13–14; 2007–8 data); TransFair Canada (2010; Canada data).

momentum in the development of Fairtrade markets, with phenomenal growth in a number of individual markets.

Notwithstanding, the market share that Fairtrade labelling has captured still makes it insignificant compared to the proportion of producers supplying conventional commercial markets. The latest comparative data on coffee (see Table 6.2) shows that while impressive, Fairtrade labelling only accounts for under 4 per cent of individual markets in ground coffee, with a slightly higher 5 per cent market share in Switzerland, 7 per cent in France, and a very exceptional 20 per cent in the UK market. Considering that Fairtrade has only entered a cross-section of the world's coffee markets, and that within these it struggles to capture more than a 4 per cent market share, it is clear that most smallholder coffee producers are still supplying the conventional market, and will not gain entry into Fairtrade unless this market grows dramatically. Indeed, even for the producers that do gain access, many are not able to sell their entire product as Fairtrade.

It is important to understand the parameters of the Fairtrade market in terms of its capacity not only to absorb new entrants, but also to cater to its existing base of suppliers. Giovannucci and Koekoek (2003, p. 39) claim that 'less than 20% of the total available Fairtrade production [for coffee] is actually purchased with a Fairtrade premium', which means that most

Table 6.2   Fairtrade market share for ground coffee in Europe and the US

Country	2000	2004	Latest year available
Austria	0.7	2.3	2 (2008)
Belgium	1.0	1.7	2.8 (2008)
Denmark	1.8	2.0	2.0 (2004)
Finland	0.3	0.4	0.4 (2004)
France	0.1	Not available	7.0 (2007)
Germany	1.0	1.0	1.5 (2007)
Ireland	0.5	2.0	3.5
Italy	0.1	Not available	0.1 (2007)
Luxembourg	3.3	Not available	3.5
Netherlands	2.7	Not available	3.0
Norway	0.3	0.9	1.4 (2007)
Sweden	0.8	<1.0	3.4 (2008)
Switzerland	3.0	6.0	5.0 (2007)
UK	1.5	20.0	Not available
US	0.2	1.8	2

Sources: Krier (2008, p. 46; 2000/2004 data); TransFair USA (2006, p. 3; USA 2000/2004 data); FAO (2009, pp. 13–14; latest year available).

of the coffee from Fairtrade-certified producers is actually sold in the conventional market. Bart Slob conducted a value chain analysis on behalf of the WFTO, EFTA and FLO, which was published in a joint publication in 2006. He also observed that growers supplying Fairtrade coffee struggled to sell their product in the Fairtrade market (Slob, 2006, p. 136), noting that 'very often, cooperatives sell only 10 to 15 per cent of their coffee under Fairtrade conditions, while the rest (85 to 90 per cent) has to be sold to intermediaries, exporters or traders in common mainstream value chains'. This warrants that an important distinction is made between production capacity (or otherwise supply) and production use in Fairtrade coffee (the extent to which supply is absorbed by the market through demand).

Despite these limitations there may be emerging prospects for Fairtrade market growth in commodities like coffee, through the phenomenon of 'south–south' trade. For example, there has been an increase in consumption in coffee-producing countries, and certainly there is a huge potential for greater consumption in coffee-producing countries in the future. Figure 6.4 compares consumption levels in Brazil to that of all the other coffee-producing countries that currently have domestic coffee markets. This shows that Brazil's consumption in particular has been rising dramatically, with a recent rise in the consumption of other producing countries, including Colombia, Ethiopia, India, Indonesia

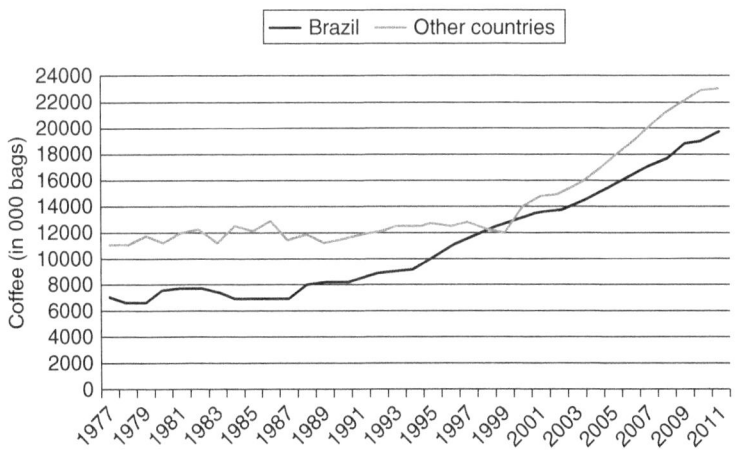

Figure 6.4 Consumption in coffee-producing countries[a]
Note:
[a] Each bag contains 60 pounds of green bean.
Sources: ICO (2007d, 2010d).

and Mexico (ICO, 2007d, 2010d). This potential of 'south–south trade', has been recognised in the Fairtrade market. Wills (Executive Director, 1997–2005) (2006, p. 21) recognises that the traditional dichotomy in fair trade relationships is one of North to South trade, claiming that 'Fair Trade started as a North–South trading relationship and still focuses on giving Southern producers access to markets in the North under fair conditions'. But times have changed, and while these opportunities have primarily emerged in handicrafts to date, 'producers are also looking for opportunities for trade with other southern countries' (Wills, 2006, p. 21). Redfern and Snedker (2002, p. 43) observe that there is a broad recognition within the Fair Trade movement '[of] the essential nature of South–South trade, including local and regional trade, in terms of market opportunities for growth of producer sales'. This may yet prove to be a device by which Fairtrade can expand its relevance beyond the market niche it currently occupies in conventional coffee markets in the consuming countries, to the as yet untapped coffee market of producing countries in the future.

Fairtrade labelling aims to provide an open system of access available for producers across all regions and countries, provided their product is listed in the Fairtrade product range. However, Fairtrade does have a stronger presence in some regions, particularly in Latin America (in terms of income) and Africa (in terms of participation levels) and it is starkly underrepresented in Asia (by all measures). These regional trends are unlikely to change significantly unless Fairtrade capacity, in terms of consumer market growth (and perhaps expansion), improves. Even then, growth of market capacity in Fairtrade will be hard-pressed to improve the productive use of current participants, let alone make room for new entrants. Essentially Fairtrade remains, to a great extent, a niche market supplied by a niche producer base with limited capacity for expansion. These market realities set high barriers of entry for producers, as do the gatekeepers for Fairtrade certification.

Producer access: Applying for Fairtrade certification

FLO-Cert (2007b) claims that '[o]ur certificate is a passport enabling access to the international markets'. It is important to remember, however, that a 'passport' only opens doors for those privileged 'citizens' that are entitled to carry it. This raises the question: how difficult is it for producers to be awarded with this certificate or passport, whereby they also gain the right of access to promised international (Fairtrade) markets? This section will focus in on the rules that govern producer access to Fairtrade coffee markets, and the application process for Fairtrade certification, including key standards which producers' organisations must meet.[3] While a Fairtrade passport may be desirable, it may remain elusive for many marginalised producers with limited resources. Essentially access to Fairtrade and its promise of international markets is limited to well-resourced and well-organised collective producers' organisations, leaving individual producers and under-resourced organisations at the wayside.

Application procedures and certification criteria

FLO-Cert clearly outlines that the purpose of the application process is (FLO-Cert, 2012d):

* to assess whether the applicant falls within the 'scope' of Fairtrade certification
* to provide applicants with sufficient information 'to properly prepare for the rest of the Certification process'
* to convey all applicable Fairtrade rules, comprising standards and certification requirements, to an applicant
* to open lines of communication between an applicant and FLO-Cert

The application process is very much a preparatory phase, designed to weed out the likely candidates from the unlikely hopefuls, through a process of information exchange that allows evaluation of the viability of an application. While the application process for certification is a fundamental first introduction for producers' organisations to Fairtrade labelling generally, it also provides the first indication of the types of resources and skills producers will need to successfully go through the process of Fairtrade certification.

'Producers' organisations must be able to meet the demands of five stages, spanning the application and certification process, before access to Fairtrade labelling can be awarded. These stages are application, audit, evaluation, certification and certification cycle (in this last stage, ongoing compliance is monitored) (FLO-Cert, 2012d). However, to even access the system, producers' organisations need to first have access to communication infrastructure (e.g. telephone, mail or Internet) or, in some cases, access to an in-country Producer Liaison Office or staff member. These lines of communication are crucial for producers' organisations in researching the scope and applicability of Fairtrade standards – for the purpose of submitting an application (by downloading or requesting an application form, and then sending the completed form by mail or email), and in order to receive additional information packages and questionnaires. In addition, as prescribed in Fairtrade standards, producers must be organised in order to be eligible to apply for certification. Table 6.3 sets out the current Fairtrade categories for small producer organisations, noting that there are two key similarities across all categories: they must be democratically controlled and by a majority small-farmer membership. This means that these organisations need to have in place mechanisms that ensure and demonstrate democratic control by the membership, including transparency (e.g. of accounts and decisions) for all members and voting by all members on key issues to the organisation. In a smaller organisational structure, such as one whose membership is drawn from a single community or village, creating and implementing mechanisms that support transparency and build trust may not be that difficult, although in a more widespread organisational structure, perhaps spanning many communities or villages, this may prove more difficult. Indeed, the key differences in Fairtrade small farmers' organisational structures primarily relate to two factors that illustrate the types of logistical challenges smallholder producers may face in creating viable Fairtrade organisational structures: these are the level of bureaucracy and the scale of the organisation.

For producers who are not already organised, creating viable organisational structures that meet Fairtrade requirements sets clear challenges. First grade organisations in many respects are the most straightforward of structures. The members are individual producers, and the levels of bureaucracy end there. However, second grade and third grade

Table 6.3   Typology of Fairtrade small producers' organisations

Organisation type	Organisational features
First grade	One-tier organisational structure Democratic control by members Small farmers make up the majority of the membership
Second grade	Two-tier organisational structure Democratic control by members Membership of first grade organisations Provision of central services to membership
Third grade	Three-tier organisational structure Democratic control by members Membership of second grade organisations Provision of central services to membership

Source: Adapted from FLO-Cert (2011, p. 4).

organisations are characterised by additional levels of grower representation and administration. While all organisational types can range in scale between less than 50 members to over 1000 members, the scale of what a single member represents in each grade of small farmers' organisations is very different. A membership of 50 in a first grade organisation simply refers to 50 smallholder producers and their families, perhaps a single village community in Papua New Guinea (PNG). A membership of 50 in a second grade organisation refers to 50 first grade organisations (which likely vary in their scale) presided over by a Central Structure, perhaps encompassing producers across a number of village communities. A membership of 50 in a third grade organisation refers to 50 second grade organisations (which can be further broken down into their respective first grade memberships and Central Structures) presided over by a Central Structure, likely spanning at least as many village communities, and perhaps representing a whole coffee-producing region.

Producer access: The cost of certification

In addition to the procedures and criteria for Fairtrade certification set out previously, producers must oversee the costs associated with Fairtrade certification. The cost of certification is absorbed by the producers and traders that participate in Fairtrade. For Fairtrade to offer opportunities for smallholder producers, it must after all, operate as a financially sustainable model. However, at what point is the price of certification too high, and what are the implications for smallholder access to the Fairtrade market?

Fairtrade costs and producer capacities

For smallholder producers' organisations to apply for, let alone gain Fairtrade certification, there are a number of fees that they must cover along the way. The fees producers are faced with range from application and initial certification fees to post-certification costs (annual fees as well as those associated with any follow-up audits which may be required) (FLO-Cert, 2011, p. 5). Fees may also vary if, for example, coverage for additional products and processing entities is required (FLO-Cert, 2011, p. 6). Costs may also be modified with, for example, organic certified organisations eligible for a fee reduction, and producers in remote areas incurring additional fees for any extra travel days required for the auditor to get there (FLO, 2011a, p. 12). Table 6.4 outlines the basic fee structure for a first grade smallholder producers' organisation. To begin with, a smallholder producers' organisation must pay an application

Table 6.4 Fairtrade first grade producer certification fees (€)

Cost category (no. of members)	Application (flat) fee	Initial certification fee	Annual audit fee
A (<50)	525	1430	1170
B (50–100)		2040	1610
C (101–250)		2250	1790
D (251–500)		2450	1970
E (501–1000)		3060	2410
F (>1000)		3470	2770

Source: Adapted from FLO-Cert (2011, pp. 5, 6 and 9).

fee, which is a flat fee of €525 per applicant, irrespective of the scale of organisation. The initial audit fee applies in the first year of certification and is charged according to the scale of organisation. In the years following certification, producers also need to pay an annual certification fee.

Table 6.5 shows that, according to these fees, a first grade organisation of fewer than 50 members would be charged €1430 in its first year (€31.77 each if there are 45 members) and one with more than 1000 members would be charged €3470 (€1.73 each if there are 2000 members). These fees are incurred for the process of gaining certification, without any guarantee that certification will be awarded. This is a high-cost risk for small organisational structure with fewer than 50. However, the price is more easily absorbed by organisations with a higher number of members. A first grade organisation of fewer than 50 members could be charged a total of €3770 over three years, representing a cost of €83.77 per member over three years (if there are 45 members). For an organisation of more than 1000 members, these figures would change to €9010 – the total costs over three years, representing €4.50 per member (if there are 2000 members). There are two important implications. First, the fee structure favours larger organisational structures; and second, small groups of individual smallholder producers are unlikely to manage the cost of certification. This is consistent with the requirement that smallholder producers must be organised to access Fairtrade markets, but it effectively adds another requirement of mass mobilisation, which is not stipulated in the standards.

Based on the preceding evaluation of costs for first grade organisations, it is already apparent that second and third grade organisations, based on the advantage of being even larger in scale, are likely to absorb certification costs more easily. Table 6.6 provides a breakdown of the

Table 6.5 Fairtrade first grade producer certification cost scenarios (three years)

Cost Category	Costs[a] (€)					
(No. of members)	First year	Second year	Third year	Total	Per member (first year)	Per member (three years)
A (45 members)	1430	1170	1170	3770	31.77	83.77
B (95 members)	2040	1610	1610	5260	21.47	55.36
C (245 members)	2250	1790	1790	5830	9.18	23.79
D (495 members)	2450	1970	1970	6390	4.94	12.90
E (995 members)	3060	2410	2410	7880	3.07	7.91
F (2000 members)	3470	2770	2770	9010	1.73	4.50

Note:
[a] Costs based on the following: first-year initial certification fee; and second- and third-year annual audit fees.
Source: Adapted from FLO-Cert (2011, pp. 5, 6, 9).

Table 6.6 Fairtrade second and third grade producer certification fees (€)

Cost category (no. of members[a])	Application fee	Initial Central Structure fee	Initial certification fee	Annual Central Structure fee	Annual audit fee
A (<50)	525	1530	920	1170	720
B (50–100)			1020		720
C (101–250)			1130		810
D (251–500)			1230		900
E (501–1000)			1530		1080
F (>1000)			1740		1250

Note:
[a] Here 'members' refers to the member organisations of the second or third grade structures. Only a sample of members is audited (this is calculated as the square root of total members, with a maximum of 20 members audited for organisations with 400 members or more).
Source: Adapted from FLO-Cert (2011, pp. 5, 8, 10, 11).

basic fee structure for first and second grade organisation spanning the application process and post-certification auditing costs. These organisations incur an additional fee for their 'central structure', which is defined by FLO-Cert (2011, p. 5) as 'the central (umbrella) organisation of a 2nd or 3rd grade organisation'. It is important to note, that only a sample of member organisations will be audited by FLO-Cert. This is calculated as the square root of total members, where a maximum of 20 organisations can be audited for second and third grade structures with more than 400 members. So, for example, a second grade organisation with 400 members would have 20 members audited at a rate of €1230 each for the initial certification fee and €900 each for the annual audit fee. There are also a number of additional fees that first, second and third grade organisations may be charged.

In addition to the basic fee structures outlined earlier, there are some extra costs that producer organisations could incur. For example, the application fee for certification of an additional product is a flat fee of €160, and for certification of additional member organisations (i.e. in the case of second- and third-tier structures), an application fee of €160 is also applied (FLO-Cert, 2011, pp. 5–6). In contrast, the initial certification fee for additional products is €210 for all organisations (FLO-Cert, 2011, pp. 6, 8). Processing installations also attract additional fees according to the labour power used. In the initial certification stage for all organisations, a processing installation requiring fewer than ten workers is charged €210, compared to €410 for those with ten–100 workers and €620 for those with more than 100 workers (FLO-Cert, 2011, p. 7). Slightly reduced annual audit fees apply for these extras as well. Considering that additional products and processing capacity would add value, these additional expenses appear modest.

In recognition of the financial obstacles producers may face, FLO itself has created a Producer Certification Fund in an effort to ensure that marginalised producers are not excluded because of the cost of certification. The fund is only open for applications from smallholder producers' organisations for the purpose of covering initial inspection fees or meeting re-inspection fees (FLO, 2012c, p. 1). As certification costs are also built into FLO's calculation of costs of sustainable production, which inform the setting of Fairtrade minimum prices (FLO Standards Unit, 2010, p. 17), there is likely an expectation that Fairtrade incomes will ultimately cover certification costs. Only eligible organisations, which can satisfy factors such as 'export capacity'; likelihood of having/finding a market for their goods; and which have not already received the grant twice can apply to the Producer Certification Fund (FLO, 2007d, pp. 1–2). Further, FLO will prioritise applications from LDCs, including coffee-producing countries like Timor Leste, Tanzania and Ethiopia, and for particular products sourced from particular origins.[4] FLO stipulates a cap on how much different types of organisations can receive, offering a maximum of 75 per cent of the certification fee for first grade organisations and a maximum of 50 per cent for that of second and third grade organisations (although 'maximum rates' are not guaranteed) (FLO, 2007d, p. 3). Certainly, this fund serves as an important avenue to improve the access that the less well-resourced smallholder producers' organisations have to Fairtrade.

In addition, producers may attract funding from other private sources. Certainly, within alternative trade networks, both start-up and long-term support is typical of both ATOs and NGOs operating in these networks (see Chapter 4). Indeed, in a recent report published by EFTA, which represents major European ATOs, a survey of producers across Africa, Asia and South America found that many were relying on external funding from a range of sources, including churches, community funding projects, international donors and banks (Boonman et al., 2011, pp. 58–9). This does raise the issue of dependence, however, which may work to undermine how open Fairtrade really is. The concern is that while producers are dependent on start-up capital and support to access Fairtrade, they may remain dependent on external supports, which are beyond their control (rather than the internal capacities within their own organisational structures and therefore within their control). Further research is needed, not only on the extent of such dependence but also whether Fairtrade income really helps to ameliorate this.

Conclusion

FLO's (2003) vision is that 'Fairtrade is the norm for poor and disadvantaged producers and workers, and a reference for all trade across the world'. The question is: can this vision be supported by the constraints and limitations on producer access to Fairtrade certification and markets? This chapter has shown that, currently, this vision falls flat. Fairtrade standards present a number of obstacles that makes access to Fairtrade labelling difficult for many smallholder producers. Cost can be a high burden for producers that struggle to put food on the table, let alone to afford close to their yearly pay packet in certification fees. Also, the requirement to mobilise into collective organisational structures immediately excludes many smallholder coffee producers, which may go towards explaining why some regions, such as Asia, are underrepresented in Fairtrade labelling.

Until FLO makes more significant headway and becomes more broadly accessible for smallholder producers – by growing the Fairtrade market, making inroads into underrepresented countries and regions, and creating greater opportunities for the most marginalised smallholder producers – it is important to recognise that the opportunities offered in Fairtrade only directly apply to the lucky few smallholder producers' organisations that have gained access.

7
Fairtrade Impacts on Coffee Producers

The claim is made on a packet of Okapa Organic *Fairtrade* coffee,[1] sourced from PNG, that '[t]he people who grew and picked this FAIRTRADE Certified coffee will directly benefit from our ethical choices by getting an above market price for their coffee and a local living wage for their efforts'. It goes on to say that 'by choosing to buy FAIRTRADE we also choose to REHUMANISE the FOOD SUPPLY chain'. This raises the question whether the claims made by Fairtrade certifiers are justified, considering the impact of Fairtrade certification on participating producers. The previous chapter qualifies this evaluation of Fairtrade's impact, with the reality that this certification is currently only accessible for a small portion of producers in the global South. Yet, Fairtrade may still serve as a model, which actors in the conventional market may aspire to. As such, it is important to ask whether Fairtrade achieves its promise of 'an above market price' and more broadly, to evaluate the opportunities this 'fair' market offers in contrast to the broader 'free' market.

This chapter explores these themes, building on the analyses of earlier chapters, and again focuses on the coffee case study. Coffee, the most mature of the Fairtrade products and beset by one of the worst commodity crises at the turn of the century, has become an even more interesting case study today. In the current climate of high market prices it clearly challenges both the sustainability, and indeed the very fairness of the Fairtrade model. Fairtrade sets both minimum prices and extra premium payments for all transactions, irrespective of the level of market prices. Across good times and bad, it has certainly offered participating producers both higher prices, but perhaps more importantly, stable prices. Yet the device of conferring a premium might be considered problematic. Indeed, it is this feature which brings the Fairtrade model – crafted under the popular motto 'trade not aid' – squarely into the arena of an 'aid' or rather 'Fairaid' model. An extra payment, in times of high market prices in particular, is difficult to defend.

The incomes that can be achieved in Fairtrade markets certainly offer significant opportunities for participating smallholder coffee producers. Yet given the ongoing limitations of Fairtrade markets, the focus in this chapter is turned on aspects of Fairtrade that may be more broadly accessible to those producers currently excluded from the Fairtrade system. To achieve this, the cooperative model, including its links with the alternative trade movement, is examined as an important area of development within and beyond Fairtrade markets.

Evaluating Fairtrade incomes

One of the strongest criticisms of free trade in coffee is that it has produced some of the lowest coffee prices in history, including levels that simply cannot sustain the livelihoods of coffee producers, let alone the level of investments needed to sustain the coffee crop. An important impact, which Fairtrade offers and free trade does not, is that it provides a sustainable income for coffee producers, which is higher than market prices when these are below sustainable production. In fact, the Fairtrade price is one of the most distinctive features of Fairtrade, compared to other sustainability certifications (including, for example, Rainforest Alliance, Utz Certified, Smithsonian Migratory Bird Certification or SMBC and Organics in coffee) that do not set a floor price. While a minimum price is a feature that may limit the appeal Fairtrade holds for conventional traders, it is also *the* feature, which arguably Fairtrade advocates most strongly defend.

In addition to minimum prices, Fairtrade also sets a premium that traders must pay to support community development in coffee-growing communities. The minimum price is a transaction price, the price that is perceived as an appropriate sale price, which adequately compensates the grower for the coffee traded. Essentially, the minimum price is intended to cover the costs of production (FLO, 2006a, p. 3). The Fairtrade premium is 'an extra payment' (FLO, 2006a, p. 3). Since the introduction of Fairtrade coffee, there have been three major changes to Fairtrade minimum prices and premiums. Until 31 May 2007 the Fairtrade premium for coffee was US$0.05 per pound, and an additional US$0.15 per pound for double certified (Fairtrade and organic) coffee (FLO, 2007e, p. 3). After this, the Fairtrade premium for both single certified (Fairtrade) and double certified (Fairtrade and organic) changed to US$0.10 per pound, and a new 'organic differential' of US$0.20 per pound was created for double-certified coffee (FLO, 2007e, pp. 4–5).[2] Then in June 2008 the minimum prices for washed and unwashed Arabica were both changed, with washed Arabica achieving an increase of 4 cents to US$1.21 per pound and unwashed Arabica an increase by 5 cents to US$1.15 per pound (FLO, 2008). Finally, in 2011, both Fairtrade minimum prices for Arabica coffee, as well as the premium and organic differential applied to all coffees was changed. From 1 April 2011, a loading of US$0.15 was added to the minimum price for both washed and unwashed Arabica, while both the organic differential and Fairtrade premium applied to all coffees was raised by US$0.10 (FLO, 2011p). Table 7.1 compares the different prices paid for coffee sold by Fairtrade producers. The real story behind Fairtrade prices, however, can be told only when comparing these to conventional prices.

Figure 7.1 compares the Fairtrade minimum price plus premium (moving between the different rates explained previously) for Arabica coffee, against the market price for a major traded Arabica bean – 'Brazilian Naturals'.[3] When the market price falls below the Fairtrade minimum price, the latter applies plus the Fairtrade premium. The *market price* plus premium applies when market prices are higher. This figure shows that Fairtrade coffee producers selling Fairtrade Arabica as a 'Brazilian Naturals' coffee often receive 50 to 70 cents more than the market rate. Comparing the Fairtrade Robusta's price structure to conventional Robusta's prices produces an even higher average price difference (see Figure 7.2). The Fairtrade price model not only keeps prices above market levels, no matter how high the market prices go, but it keeps prices stable, addressing the issue of volatility in coffee prices for its niche market members. It is both the features of stable prices and additional

Table 7.1   Fairtrade coffee prices and premiums from April 2011 (US cents/lb)

	Minimum price Fairtrade certified	Organic differential for Fairtrade/Organic certified	Fairtrade premium
Washed Arabica	140	+ 30	+ 20
Unwashed Arabica	135		
Washed Robusta	105		
Unwashed Robusta	101		

Sources: Adapted from FLO (2010b, 2011p).

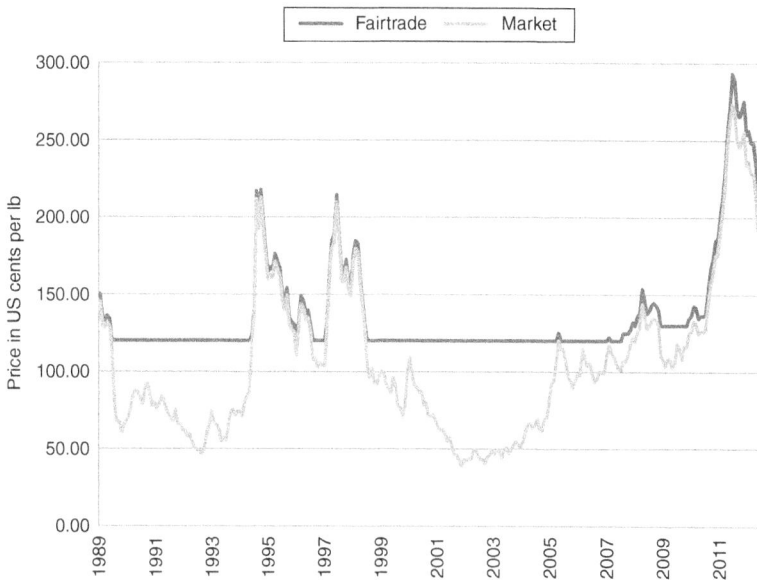

Figure 7.1 Fairtrade and market prices for Brazilian Naturals (1989–2012)
Sources: ICO (2007b, 2007d, 2010a, 2012); FLO (2007e, 2010c).

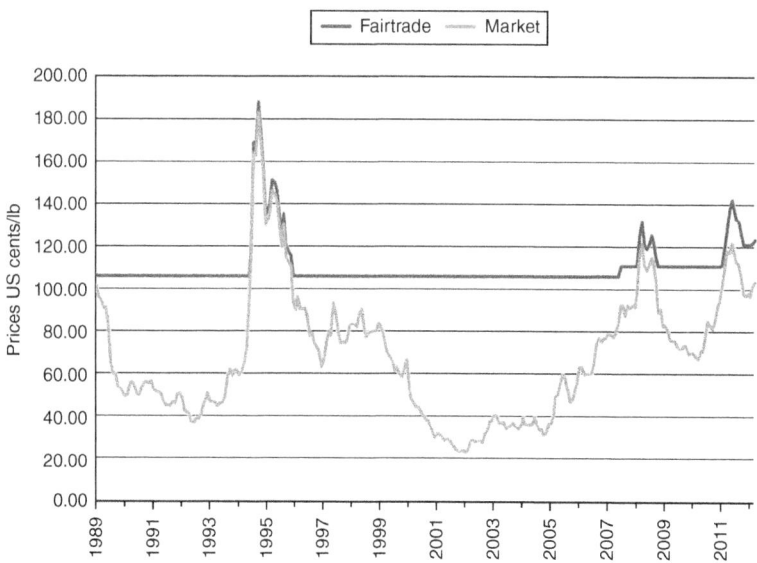

Figure 7.2 Fairtrade and market prices for Robusta (1989–2012)
Sources: ICO (2007b, 2007d, 2010a, 2012); FLO (2007e, 2010c).

income, which make the Fairtrade market so attractive for marginalised and impoverished coffee producers.

Fairtrade prices, depending on the percentage of coffee that a Fairtrade producers' organisation can sell as Fairtrade, can represent a significant increase in income for smallholder producers that participate in Fairtrade. Eshuis and Harmsen (2003) estimate that over a 15-year period, Fairtrade prices and premiums awarded to smallholder coffee producers supplying the Dutch market – the first Fairtade coffee market – represented approximately €47 million in additional income (see Figure 7.3). In the US market, one of the strongest Fairtrade markets today, producers received just under $17 million through Fairtrade premium payments in 2011, over three times as much as that received in 2007 (see Figure 7.4). It is this maintenance of additional income even during times where market prices are high, which aids the longevity of the Fairtrade model, despite the difficulty in defending additional payments under such market conditions.

The Fairtrade model is especially relevant for producers when the conventional market does not pay a sustainable price. When market prices across the board are higher, the incentive for producers to sell via Fairtrade is removed. FLO recognises this limitation and the impact on the sustainability of its supply base. FLO (2011o, p. 41) attributes a drop in the share of coffee sales as a percentage of total Fairtrade sales as most likely caused by high market prices, which 'have made alternatives to Fairtrade more attractive during this time period'. The Fairtrade premium is thus an important incentive for producers to remain within the Fairtrade model in times of high market prices.

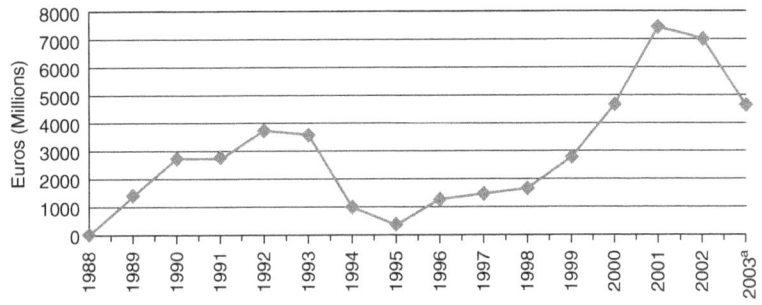

Figure 7.3   Additional producer income in Dutch Fairtrade market (1988–2003[a])
Note:
[a] Estimates up until mid-November.
Source: Eshuis and Harmsen (2003, p. 29).

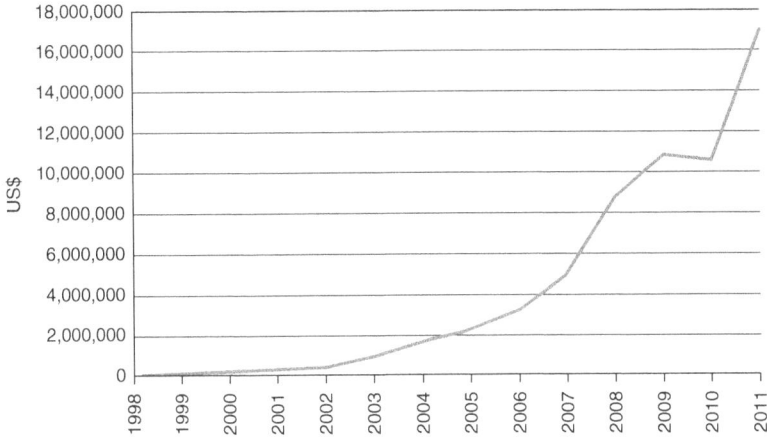

Figure 7.4 Fairtrade premium paid in US market (1998–2011)
Source: Fair Trade USA (2011, p. 19).

Fairtrade or 'Fairaid': The Fairtrade premium

Currently, Fairtrade's impact in coffee-growing communities is primarily delivered through the Fairtrade premium. The premium serves as an 'extra payment' designed to help producers improve their lives. As such, it flouts the general premise upon which Fairtrade operates – to redefine trade exchanges to properly reflect the value of production – as it asks buyers to pay a levy above the product price in times where the product price is considered sustainable for producers. Essentially, it could be considered an aid payment. Yet, this built-in 'Fairaid' payment has proven critical to producer capacity to regenerate and build their businesses.

It is defined by FLO (2011o, p. 51) as 'a flexible support that farmers and workers can use to meet their specific needs and those of their communities'. Unlike the minimum price, which is determined according to the costs of production, premium use is driven by producers, whether they are organised as producers or as hired labour. FLO has observed trends in premium spending for both producers' organisations and plantations with hired labour towards spending in areas such as 'community', 'education', the 'environment', 'health' and 'gender equity' (FLO, 2011o, pp. 51–2). Producers' organisations also spend their premium on investments in 'business development' and 'production and processing', as well as other uses which include, for example, direct payments to members (FLO, 2011o, p. 51). For workers, investments in 'capacity building and career development', as well as 'other supports' which include, for example, provision of childcare, loans and housing are also observed (FLO, 2011o, p. 52).

Table 7.2 provides a breakdown of the use of the additional income generated by the Fairtrade premium for 2009–10. It examines expenditure by smallholder and contract production organisations by all Fairtrade products and for coffee specifically. Coffee producers accounted for the largest portion of the Fairtade premium pie, using up 34 per cent compared to the 24 per cent use by banana producers and then less than 10 per cent for all other products (FLO, 2011o, p. 47). The data in Table 7.2 indicates that reinvestment in business development (at the organisational level) and production and processing (at the farm level) are key priorities for producer organisations, accounting for just over 50 per cent of the expenditure for all products, and just under 50 per cent for coffee. The value of some of the premium for Fairtrade coffee producers can be seen in Table 7.3. It can include investments such as mobile medical clinics, processing machines and an adult education programme.

Interestingly, the Premium expenditure category of 'Other' accounts for approximately one-third of all premium expenditure across the board. This category is defined by FLO (2011o, p. 51) as including, for example, 'cash payments and other forms of direct financial or social support'. FLO (2011o, p. 52) directly links a growth in this category

Table 7.2 Fairtrade premium use (2009–10)

Expenditure category	All products (%)	Coffee (%)
Community	7	4
Education	4	2
Environment	3	2
Health	3	1
Gender Equity	0	0
Investment in business development[a]	24	30
Investment in production and processing[a]	30	28
Other	28	29
Not known	1	4

Note:
[a] Investment in business development expenditure is at the level of Fairtrade producer organisations, while investment in production and processing is at the farm level.
Source: FLO (2011o, pp. 54, 59).

Table 7.3 Fairtrade premium use: Selected coffee-growing communities

Origin[a]	Nicaragua	Colombia	Peru	Guatemala
No. of members	524	125	1120	260
Health	Mobile medical clinics, water filters Targeting women's health	–	25% of Fairtrade premium goes to a health care programme; pays 50% of health care costs of its members	Improvements to nutrition and medical services
Education	–	Funds five scholarships each year for a local university; purchases school supplies for the children of cooperative members	–	Adult education programme; elementary school built
Infrastructure	–	'Purchase of new de-pulping machines and wet processing tanks'	Helps members purchase depulpers (through a loan scheme)	–
Technical supports	Training, to improve cup quality, in environmental protection	Training for pest control/ fertilisation and to change to organic production	Include assistance in improving coffee quality and for 'social and business development projects'	Provides training in organic production techniques
Credit supports	Lending programme with loans for 218 women	'Solidarity Fund' to support members in need (e.g. urgent medical care, disaster relief)	Pre-harvest finance for all members and loans for farm maintenance	–
Special projects	–	Sponsors an exporting business, to build export and local roasting capacity	Installs solar panels Trains cooperative 'leaders' to undertake internal inspections against organic standards	Social programme to empower women

Note:
[a] Cooperative names/acronyms as listed on FLO website are Aldea Global (Nicaragua), ACOC (Colombia), Bagua Grande (Peru) and ADIPCO (Guatemala).
Source: FLO (2006b).

of expenditure to an increase in direct payments made to members, which it attributes to 'the rise in commodity prices which has made it much more challenging for cooperatives to buy sufficient supply from their members'. This raises a question of the sustainability of the Fairtrade model when it no longer remains necessary or attractive to producers once the market performs. It surely raises an ethical issue when Fairtrade's own producers have to be arguably 'bought off' for continued loyalty, and likely undermines the product assurance given to consumers that they are supporting the payment of fair prices for the products they purchase. It is, in any event, of concern that such payments have impacted on premium use across the remaining categories, as the value realised by communities for expenditures in areas such as health and education has been invaluable.

While the device of the premium could be labelled as 'Fairaid' and therefore, unsustainable, the use of the premium for community-based projects in Fairtrade requires the construct of a collective organisational structure, such as a cooperative, which allows the community collectively to identify and take ownership of community priorities for premium use. Collective organisational structures such as cooperatives and the opportunities they offer, however, are not limited to Fairtrade networks. While they may be a feature of Fairtrade, collective organisational structures predate and extend beyond Fairtrade markets and are more broadly accessible for producers outside the confines of the Fairtrade model. Unlike the 'quasi-aid' premise of the Fairtrade premium they may work as a 'self-help' model for producers.

Self-help in Fairtrade: The cooperative model

This section will examine arguments for employing the cooperative model as a development tool in agricultural production, and examines, as an example, opportunities that the cooperative model presently, but also potentially, offers smallholder coffee producers in PNG.

Fairtrade dictates that participating marginalised producers – with the exception of hired labour – organise into collective organisational structures like cooperatives. A cooperative is defined by the International Cooperative Alliance (ICA,[4] 2005–11) as 'an autonomous association of persons united voluntarily to meet their common economic, social, and cultural needs and aspirations through a jointly-owned and democratically-controlled enterprise'. Before the uptake in the Fair Trade movement of the cooperative model, this model has long been seen as an important tool for development, and has also had a long history in coffee-producing countries. Gertler (2001, p. 6) refers to the multidimensionality of cooperatives: the capacity of the cooperative model to combine 'multiple economic, social and ecological objectives'. He highlights features of cooperatives, showing this model as appropriate for smallholder development. The promotion of 'cooperation and collective action', the 'sharing of the costs and benefits', 'economic democracy and the empowerment of marginalised groups', and the 'organisational capacity for communication, training, and education' through cooperative structures (Gertler, 2001, p. 6), are all in theory features that provide a collective (cooperative) of smallholder producers with important capacities that they do not have as individual smallholder units.

Promotion of the 'cooperative' model in Papua New Guinea

The potential for the cooperative model to serve as a vehicle for development is recognised by the PNG regulatory authority for cooperative formation. The 'Office of the Cooperative Societies' (OCS), under the Department of Trade and Industry,[5] is responsible for sanctioning the formation of 'Cooperative Societies' in PNG. The OCS (n.d.) considers the cooperative model as particularly valuable for the 'rural populace, which is generally poor [and] have few resources to get into economic activities'. In fact, PNG's Cooperative Societies are seen as an important tool through which individuals, collectively, can pool their resources and build capacities that alone they could not hope for (Cooperative Societies Unit/Ministry of Trade and Industry, n.d.).

The OCS (n.d.) outlines six 'major advantages' for cooperative members in PNG that are outlined in Table 7.4. The table draws important links between the opportunities identified by the OCS as intrinsic to the cooperative model, and the relevance of these features to coffee production in PNG. One of the key features identified is the function of 'resource mobilisation', which a cooperative structure promotes and enables. The resources that can be collectively mobilised begin with the labour power of smallholder coffee producers themselves. The pooling of financial capital may enable investments, like road repairs or the purchase of vehicles for transportation, which exceed the possibilities of individual incomes. It offers opportunities to 'upgrade' through pooling resources, thereby building capacity to undertake additional processing and in some cases exporting, distinguishing the cooperative model as an important opportunity for smallholder coffee producers.

The cooperative structure alone, without the benefit of the Fairtrade premium, can harness many of the results, in terms of community development, which Fairtrade labelling tries to achieve. This becomes

Table 7.4 PNG's cooperative Societies: Opportunities for smallholder coffee producers

Cooperative Societies Unit: Benefits of the cooperative model	Opportunities for smallholder coffee producers
1. Employment Members of a cooperative are instantly 'self-employed', as they will 'reap the economic and social gains' generated by their participation in a cooperative	Stable employment opportunity, where the prospects of the individual are tied to that of the collective (thus, individual economic and social gain mobilised by *collective action*)
2. Resource mobilisation Opportunities to mobilise resources through a collective, which individuals alone cannot facilitate	Smallholder coffee producers may be able to mobilise important resources such as financial capital, which in turn may mobilise resources (through spending) such as tools, fertiliser, transportation, road improvements, housing, education and health resources, etc
3. Better prices It is expected that prices received by producers will increase Producers in a cooperative can cut out middlemen like 'roadside buyers' by selling directly to exporters or exporting themselves	Cooperatives may remove dependence on middlemen by developing their own capacities in areas such as processing and transportation. Thus, coffee producers will no longer need to sacrifice the additional value gained in these stages, or to trust that middleman prices are fair
4. Import/export capacity Cooperative structures, which meet the relevant requirements, 'will be issued with import and export licenses', and potentially gain direct access not only to export into international markets, but also to import processing equipment from outside of PNG	Cooperatives have the potential to 'upgrade' in the coffee processing and trading chain. By building capacity to process to 'green bean' (smallholders typically sell their coffee only as 'cherry' or have the tools to process to 'parchment'), producers can sell direct to exporters, or even export themselves
5. Reduction of land conflicts and under-utilisation It is expected that cooperatives can reduce land conflicts and be more productive with their use of land resources	Improving the viability and profitability of coffee production through cooperatives may promote greater productivity in coffee. A collective identity through cooperatives may reduce disputes over land
6. Facilitates national economic development PNGs economy will be positively impacted by the perceived greater production capacity (better outputs) of cooperatives, especially in commodities for export	Coffee is the only source of cash income for most Papua New Guineans – strengthening coffee exports can add greatly to the national 'purse' but also improve the livelihoods of PNG citizens – economically and socially

Source: Column one adapted from Cooperative Societies Unit/Ministry of Trade and Industry (n.d.).

apparent in a comparison of four cooperatives in PNG. Table 7.5 canvasses key features of three smallholder coffee producers' cooperatives,[6] one of which (HOAC) supplies the Fairtrade and organic coffee markets. HOAC has made important improvements within its own communities, largely through the support of its export partner (Coffee Connections) but also through the additional finance provided by the Fairtrade premium, which is available for community investments. This has provided extra funding for education, health and infrastructure projects.

The two smallholder cooperatives presented in column one and two do not supply any certified coffee market. However, by pooling their resources, they have made significant achievements within their own communities. Producers in Cooperative A have created 30ha of 'communal coffee growing', in addition to individual plots, where the cooperative members join their labour power to grow, harvest, and market coffee in order to generate additional income for the community.[7] A grower from Producers Cooperative B claims that 'self-reliance is really important to us . . . it is where we draw our strength' and rejects any external funding. Independently, the cooperative is building an elementary school (with help from a former member). It is also staffing the school with its own members, who have passed through a community teacher programme in PNG. All of these examples show that collective organisational structures, such as cooperatives, may offer unique opportunities for smallholder coffee producers, even without the added benefit of the premium that Fairtrade suppliers receive. In fact, while access to the Fairtrade market is limited, the opportunities that collective organisational structures may offer to the majority of smallholder coffee producers that supply the conventional market, in terms of resource mobilisation and community development generally, cannot be overstated.

The cooperative model provides a powerful tool for smallholder producers, which can generate opportunities even without being linked to Fairtrade markets, not least because joining a cooperative is not constrained by factors such as market size or cost. The fact that smallholder producers are thereby pooling their labour and resources enables them to develop and execute community development priorities. It also allows them to mitigate the problem of being a smallholder in a big pool of multinationals, by joining into slightly 'bigger fish' as cooperative entities. This illustrates one of the most powerful uses of the cooperative model, as noted by Gertler (2001, p. 5) who claims that '[c]ooperatives have often come into existence because small-scale producers seek protection from more powerful players in the market-place'. This ability to better leverage their position in the market is bolstered

Table 7.5 Smallholder coffee producers' cooperatives in Papua New Guinea: 2004

	Producers Cooperative A	Producers Cooperative B	HOAC (Fairtrade/Organic)
Number of members	100 members	105 families	2600 producers
Decision-making structure	Formal structure, including village leader	Formal structure, including a 'top committee' (village leader is permanent member), 'book of rules' and village magistrate	Formal structure, including positions of chairman and secretary. Holds general assembly where the cooperative members make decisions on community projects (e.g. on spending Fairtrade premium)
Forms of income[a]	Coffee, some fish	Coffee, vanilla, fish; selling bread at local market and cultural/dance activities	Coffee
Coffee processing	Sell 50:50 parchment to cherry[b]	Process to parchment, pay factory to process to green bean	Process to parchment
Coffee marketing chain	Group marketing: sell to PNGCGF, which sells to Coffee Pacifica	Middlemen used to drive in to pick up coffee cherry but there have been too many hold-ups	Exporter, Coffee Connections, organises processing to green bean, undertakes conditioning/sorting of coffee and exports into organic/Fairtrade market for HOAC
Community projects	30ha of communal land for communal growing/harvesting/marketing of coffee	Building an elementary school in the community, which was 'donated by ex-member' – using teachers from the community (there is a community teacher programme in PNG)	Through additional income from the Fairtrade premium the cooperative has purchased desks and books for schools and medicines and mattresses for the health centres. With support from Coffee Connections have been rebuilding a vital road

Funding/supports	Trying to get funding from AusAID to buy new hand depulping machines	The community doesn't have or want any outside funding. Has been waiting for over a year to get training for health care in the community	Coffee Connections has provided financial support (covered initial costs of certification, paid for road improvements) and technical advice. Wildlife Conservation Group has provided technical advice
Goals	Diversify into vanilla, livestock and vegetable farming	Diversify into cocoa	To get shade grown certification – Rainforest Alliance and Smithsonian Migratory Bird Certification

Note:

[a] Smallholder producers in the cooperatives are also subsistence producers of basic food necessities and coffee is the primary source of cash income.

[b] A problem with the depulping method is that often a lot of the beans are damaged or rotten after depulping but they have no other options.

Sources: Producers Cooperative A (Cooperative Leader A, 2004), Producers Cooperative B (Cooperative Leader B, 2004), HOAC (Ame, 2006) and interviews with smallholder coffee producers in Starr (n.d.).

not only through resource mobilisation in production but also through the potential for new networking opportunities with actors in consumer markets.

Opportunities in cooperative networks

In addition to its value as an organisational tool for smallholder production, forming a cooperative can also lead to networking opportunities for smallholders. The cooperative network is extensive, drawing on a membership of 'over 800 million people around the world' (ICA, 2009). The cooperative tradition is strong both in developed and developing countries. In the US 25 per cent of the population belong to a cooperative and in Germany 20 million people are members of a cooperative (ICA, 2009). In Colombia, 10.7 per cent of the population belongs to a cooperative and coffee cooperatives 'are responsible for 35.29% of Colombian coffee production', while for the biggest coffee producer, Brazil, 'cooperatives are responsible for 40% of the agricultural GDP' (ICA, 2009). As '[t]he cooperative model of enterprise can be applied to any business activity' (ICA, 2007), this means that producer cooperatives can potentially gain access to a wide range of cooperative enterprises, including important support organisations.

Some of the sectors in which cooperatives operate, aside from agriculture, include the consumer sector, banking and credit sector, and the health sector (ICA, 2007). These are all potentially relevant for producer cooperatives. Again in PNG, cooperatives have taken three forms: the 'Marketing Cooperatives' (smallholder cooperatives which build resources to store, transport and market predominantly cash-crops like coffee); 'Consumer Cooperatives' (providing a retail space for the sale of basic goods, with any profits paid to members in dividends); and 'Credit Cooperatives' (through which Marketing Cooperatives can obtain credit to grow their business on better terms than those offered by traditional banks) (Cooperative Societies Unit/Ministry of Trade and Industry, n.d.). An example of a cooperative in the banking/credit sector that assists coffee producers is the Dutch cooperative, the 'Rabobank Foundation'. In conjunction with the 'Green Development Foundation', it has provided support to '122.000 coffee producers in 7 Central-American countries', providing 'support to the credit divisions of the farmers' cooperatives' and also supporting Fair Trade through 'risk-bearing capital and trade financing' (Develtere and Pollet, 2005, p. 18). Cooperatives in consumer markets also play an important role in supporting producers through Fair Trade. In fact, in consumer markets like the UK, Italy and Switzerland, cooperative retail outlets such as supermarkets have been important outlets for Fair Trade products (Develtere and Pollet, 2005, p. 17). The links between cooperatives and Fair Trade are examined in the following section.

Cooperatives in Fair Trade networks

There is a clear link between the Fair Trade movement and the cooperative movement, evident in the importance of the cooperative model to, in particular, ATOs and their networks. Certainly there are parallels between integrated cooperative networks and integrated alternative trade networks. In fact, there is often an overlap between the two. On the one hand, the cooperative model is an important organisational structure in production for Fair Trade, but it can also be applied in the various stages of air (or alternative) trading chains. On the other hand, the International Cooperative Alliance (ICA, 2010) recognises that Fair Trade provides important opportunities for cooperatives to enhance their competitiveness in producing and consuming sectors. The importance of the cooperative model to alternative trade networks indicates important opportunities for smallholder coffee producers in both cooperative trade and Fair Trade.

The cooperative model predates the introduction of the alternative trade model by over 100 years. The first burst of cooperative activity began in England in 1844 with the founding of 'the first modern cooperative business' – 'the Rochdale Equitable Pioneers Society' – a producer cooperative of a small collective of cotton weavers (ICA, 2005). As cooperatives evolved, the model was quickly extended to the consumer sector as well as a range of other sectors, including 'service providers' (Develtere and Pollet, 2005, p. 12). Today, cooperatives are described as being 'based on the values of self-help, self-responsibility, democracy, equality, equity and solidarity' (ICA, 2005–11). The principle of solidarity advocates 'Cooperation among Cooperatives' and accordingly aims to 'strengthen the cooperative movement through local, national, regional and international structures' (ICA, 2005–11). Solidarity is also a defining principle for ATOs, who also prefer ATO-to-ATO trade and have worked together to build formal representative structures at national, regional and international levels. However, unlike the cooperative movement which today maintains an arguably equally strong focus on consumers relative to producers, ATOs remain very producer focussed in their take on solidarity, as guided by their beginning in the charitable works of pioneering NGOs. Arguably, ATOs today fulfil a quasi 'development AID' role.

One of the important differences between the orientation of the cooperative movement and that of the alternative trade movement lies in differences in the commitment to producers, relative to consumers, a point which is eloquently made by Develtere and Pollet (2005, p. 12) who claim that 'the cooperative movement aims to increase the incomes of *consumers and producers in both North and South*, whereas the fair-trade movement in the first place wants to improve the income situation of *producers in the South'*. In this respect, Develtere and Pollet (2005, p. 13) make a compelling observation that, while 'cooperatives thrive on a logic that combines market forces with self-help, [F]air- [T]rade is driven by a support or assistance logic'. In fact, it is perhaps the insertion of the cooperative model into production for alternative trade markets, which has added that missing element of producer 'self-help' into the otherwise mainly assistance or quasi 'AID'-driven alternative trade model. Whether forming a cooperative achieves access to a Fairtrade market or not, many would argue that smallholder producers can already gain important benefits simply by forming a cooperative. Certainly they are better positioned to gain access to holistic cooperative trade networks.

Smallholder producers' organisations in alternative and cooperative trade

A good example of an integrated cooperative and alternative trade network in coffee is that of a cooperative importer, Cooperative Coffees (CC), and its network. In this example the cooperative and alternative trade model is applied holistically across all aspects of the coffee trade where possible, from production to consumption, comprising the production, export, import, roasting and retail sectors of the trade. This case study exemplifies the importance of two-tier cooperatives in building a highly integrated trading chain.

With members in both the USA and Canada, Cooperative Coffees (2010) is an importing cooperative of green coffee with a membership of 23 coffee roasters. It is also a cooperative with a clear mission to 'build and support fair and sustainable trade relationships for the benefit of farmers and their exporting cooperatives, families and communities (Cooperative Coffees, 2010). Essentially, CC functions as a second grade cooperative through which its small roasting cooperative members join forces and build an importing capacity that, as individual organisations, they could not support. The 'Members' Operating Covenant' for CC contains the explanation that individually the roasting cooperatives could not support the volume of trade they needed to 'import directly (one of the main tenants of Fair Trade) from a variety of coffee farmer cooperatives' (Cooperative Coffees, 2010). This illustrates the importance placed in alternative trade networks on supporting Fair

Trade with smallholder producers, through direct trading relationships. The cooperative model facilitates this goal by providing individual roasting operations the opportunity to build a capacity collectively, to support the direct trading relationships they desire but couldn't support individually.

Within these direct trading relationships, the individual members of CC apply a holistic approach to engendering Fair Trade values throughout their supply chains, which go above and beyond the commitment of most conventional businesses. While conventional companies purchase Fairtrade-labelled coffee in compliance with set minimum prices and premiums for Fairtrade and Fairtrade/Organic certified coffees, the members of CC work according to contracts that set significantly higher prices (Kornell, 2007, p. 12). In 2007, CC president Bill Harris confirmed that many contracts actually delivered a higher price (Kornell, 2007, p. 12). However, the additional supports that CC members provide their suppliers goes beyond a financial reward. The approach in the case of Dean's Beans is to build direct and personal relationships through which the individual needs of suppliers can be recognised and facilitated (Byers and Cycon,[8] 2004, p. 7).

Support of the development projects of its suppliers is largely funded through Dean's Beans 'Profit Sharing Program'. In addition to the Fairtrade/Organic price of US$1.41, the cooperative has 'added a six-cent Social Equity Premium paid back to the farmers for each pound of their coffee that we roast and sell' (Dean's Beans, 2010a). This has resulted in project-based investments in Dean's Beans supplier cooperatives, including start-up finance for a 'new honey business' in Peru (which has received US$2700 through this premium); the purchase of 'five water buffalo for eco-management' in Sumatra (which has received $2250 through this premium); the purchase of '14 hand de-pulping machines' in Papua New Guinea (which has received US$2800 through this premium); and the purchase of 'medicine for rural clinics in coffee area' in Timor Leste (which has received US$1000 through this premium) (Dean's Beans, 2010a). Through its profit-sharing programme, Dean's Beans has directly created opportunities for smallholder coffee producers' organisations to diversify production (Peru), promote improved environmental management (Sumatra), upgrade by building processing capacity (PNG) and invest in the health of the broader community (Timor Leste).

In integrated ATO/cooperative networks, including in the example given, networking with like-minded actors in consumer markets can offer a range of additional supports over the primarily price and premium transfers offered in Fairtrade labelling. This underscores the importance for Fair Trade to challenge the structure and behaviour of businesses, not only in producing countries but also in consumer markets.

Conclusion

Fair trade has offered valuable opportunities for smallholder producers. For those that are able to access Fairtrade markets, it offers additional income through minimum prices and premiums. Indeed, Fairtrade premiums offer important opportunities for smallholder coffee producers and their communities to invest in community development, although the recent diversion of premium payments to lure producers to continue to supply Fairtrade during high market prices underscores the vulnerability of the Fairtrade model. Also, for the bulk of smallholder coffee producers that remain excluded from this niche market, Fair Trade cannot, and probably will not, offer any direct benefits beyond the influence it can exert on the conscience of the broader business and consuming community. For the majority of smallholder coffee producers that grow a crop that is destined almost exclusively for the export market, there are widely more accessible opportunities to be realised in joining into a collective organisational structure like a cooperative model. However, Fair Trade in coffee, through Fairtrade labelling, does not appear to deliver broad opportunities for smallholder coffee producers, and one of the key sticking points relates to the terms of engagement it offers conventional businesses.

8
Ethical Consumption: Revolution from Within?

The limitation of the Fairtrade market – which ironically is an effort at mainstreaming – has clearly shown the importance for change in the conventional commercial market. The 'fairness' of ethical initiatives like Fairtrade might appear limited when measured by levels of producer participation. Therefore its capacity to transform global trade relations is compromised, raising a key concern with Fairtrade. Rather than impacting on the behaviour of participating consumers and businesses, does Fairtrade merely invite both to do their part and ease their guilt in a very limited way, without addressing or challenging the persistent problems in conventional trade rules? Conversely, do trends in Fairtrade consumption and that of other ethical initiatives suggest a broader capacity to transform the global trade regime? In turn, is this evidenced in the behaviour of corporate actors participating in Fairtrade, who by the logic of the market, should be guided by consumer preferences?

This chapter problematises the role of two important actors in the conventional marketplace: the consumer and the corporation. The first section examines the development of the ethical consumer phenomenon, both as a concept but also in terms of associated practices. This section also examines some of the potential limitations of ethical consumption regarding, for example, the universality of principles and the tension between competing ethical issues. In the second section the influence of (ethical) consumers is examined through the 'one dollar, one vote' thesis. In particular, the debate regarding consumer influence over corporate actors is examined. Finally, the chapter concludes with an examination of the strength and limitations of corporate and consumer transformations in the Fairtrade coffee market.

Fairtrade asks consumers to 'vote with their dollars', yet it is not clear whether votes via Fairtrade or ethical consumption generally greatly impact on the conduct of corporate actors, which so heavily influence the operation of the conventional marketplace. Irrespective of the impact on corporations, it is also not clear whether initiatives like Fairtrade have fostered a meaningful shift in (ethical) consumer behaviour. While some of these concerns are difficult to investigate, this chapter sets out some of the issues that might inform further discussion and research on the value of Fairtrade. Despite limited quantitative impacts on producers, if Fairtrade plays a part in a qualitative change in the conscience of consumers and/or corporations, then there may yet be the potential for greater impact on producers in the future, through contributing to a strengthening and applied critique of conventional market practices. The growth of the broader sustainability market in coffee may be a case in point.

The ethical consumer phenomenon

Mayo (2005, p. xvii) poignantly observes that '[w]hile radical artists . . . were turning ordinary objects into art, the ethical consumer pioneers were turning them into activism'. In an age of mass consumerism – with society veritably transformed by an increasing consumer culture – it may come as no surprise that consumption has become an important political space, serving as a site for consumer activism. Increasingly, ethical concerns attach to processes of market exchange, through the ethical consumption phenomenon. This section examines the concept of ethical consumption and the many issues that ethical consumers take on board. It also problematizes this phenomenon by examining some of the competing values, the issue of market information and the problem of ownership of the concept.

Defining the 'ethical consumer'

The role of consumption is no longer understood in purely economic terms. Not only is consumption one of the key drivers of many economies (Dickinson and Carsky, 2005, p. 26) but social transactions have also arguably become transformed through the rise of 'consumer culture'. Hansen and Schrader (1997, p. 443) argue that the importance of consumers cannot be reduced to statistics on the quantitative growth of consumption. Rather a qualitative change has occurred where 'people see themselves and are seen as consumers in more and more spheres of their lives' (Hansen and Schrader, 1997, p. 443). We no longer consume commodities alone, rather the principles of market economics pervade society so that even health and educational institutions have transformed into service providers, and their patients and students valued 'customers' (Hansen and Schrader, 1997, p. 443). This raises the question, how can we best understand the role of the humble consumer and of the 'art' of consumption itself?

Consumption is traditionally theorised by economists. Here the key explanatory framework is that of 'consumer sovereignty', whereby consumers are understood to direct production in a market economy through their purchasing decisions (Hansen and Schrader, 1997, p. 443). In turn, 'rational choice theory' is used to explain consumer decision-making, wherein consumers are understood to strive to maximise their 'utility' based on their 'self-interest' (Dickinson and Carksy, 2005, p. 27). However, the appropriateness of economic modelling of consumption and of consumer behaviour is now questioned on a number of levels. The internal logic of such models has been criticised, with concern that consumers lack the necessary information to make 'rational' decisions for their purchases, and therefore the capacity to either satisfy their self-interest or direct production. In turn, as consumption impacts collective welfare through the 'externalities' associated with the production of some goods (such as human rights abuses or environmental degradation), individual utility is found wanting as an organising principle for consumption (Hansen and Schrader, 1997, p. 453). Consumption has also been theorised in different ways, with concepts such as the 'consumer vote' (in the interest of communities) competing with that of (individual) 'utility maximisation' (Dickinson and Carsky, 2005, pp. 25–6). Indeed, the rise of ethical consumption itself is simply incongruent with a formula that sees purchasing decisions divorced from ethical concerns (Harrison et al., 2005, pp. 1–2). Hansen and Schrader (1997, p. 443) argue that an increasingly 'consumer society' brings with it the notion of 'consumer responsibility' and that this prompts the need for a 'modern *model of consumption*', which can better articulate and guide consumer behaviour.

Ethical consumption has been defined as 'personal consumption where the choice of a product or service exists which supports a particular ethical issue – be it human rights, the environment or animal welfare' (Cooperative Bank cited in Low and Davenport, 2007, p. 336). The concept of the ethical consumer certainly moves understanding of consumption beyond economic imperatives. Harrison (2005, p. 66) goes so far as to say that the notion of 'consumer responsibility . . . has helped to restore to consumption the idea of citizenship'. This reinforces the idea that consumption has become a site not just for purchasing, but purchasing 'votes' as well. Certainly ethical consumers are understood to apply additional criteria to those of price and quality in their purchasing decisions, with concerns reaching beyond self-interest to 'the external world around them' (Harrison et al., 2005, p. 2). Two defining features of ethical consumption emerge: a concern with the social consequences of consumption, embracing collective and external interests; and a belief that consumption can have a positive impact on these issues. What then falls within the ambit of ethical consumption?

The scope of ethical consumption

Lang and Gabriel (2005) trace the history of ethical consumption and put forward a four-wave theory on consumer activism, differentiating between 'cooperative consumers' (first wave), 'value for money consumers' (second wave), 'Naderism' (third wave) and 'alternative consumerism' (fourth wave). Cooperative and alternative consumption have already been discussed in earlier chapters. Both set clear challenges to capitalist consumption (Lang and Gabriel, 2005). In contrast, 'value for money consumers' seek greater efficiency in the market, aim to empower consumers through information and education, and strive 'to act effectively' (Lang and Gabriel, 2005, p. 45). Naderism emphasises the availability of 'free and fair' information for consumers (Lang and Gabriel, 2005, p. 45). This four-wave typology underscores the diversity in ethical consumer principles and practices.

Barnett et al. (2005, p. 21) differentiate between two distinct but related concepts: 'ethics of consumption' and 'ethical consumption'. The former problematises consumption itself and is applied in, for example, debates over the environment and sustainable consumption, which are concerned with the limits of consumption (Barnett et al., 2005, p. 21). The latter is understood as a 'medium for moral and political action', thereby necessitating more consumption, not less (Barnett et al., 2005, p. 21). In contrast, Low and Davenport (2007, pp. 340) deconstruct the scope of ethical consumption by identifying a 'triple bottom line' of defining issues. They argue that ethical consumers are concerned with one or more of the following 'ethical baselines': human rights, animal welfare and environmental welfare (Low and Davenport, 2007, p. 341). Arguably, environmental welfare falls most strongly into the 'ethics of consumption' category, while human rights in particular are more strongly supported by 'ethical consumption'. A range of consumer practices supports the pursuit of these ethical concerns.

Harrison et al. (2005, p. 3) identify five categories of ethical consumer practices, which can be further sorted into 'product'- and 'company'-oriented purchasing: boycotts, positive buying, fully screened, relationship purchasing, anti-consumerism or sustainable consumerism. For example, boycotting of a product or company can be used to advance a human rights cause. Boycotts – a negative form of consumer voting – can be distinguished from buycotts – a positive form of consumer voting (Dickinson and Carsky, 2005, p. 30). Fairtrade, of course, falls into the latter category. Irving et al. (2002) outline a spectrum of ethical consumption initiatives, employing a range of these devices. For example, ethical consumers concerned with animal welfare have undertaken boycotts and buycotts, including a boycott of Heinz in the US in the 1990s to protest the killing of dolphins through the use of 'purse-sein' nets for fishing tuna, boycotts of products and companies which used animal testing and the purchasing (or buycotting) of organic and free range foods (Irving et al., 2002).

The capacity of ethical consumption to meet its objectives faces clear challenges. Consuming in one's own self-interest is difficult enough without adding to this the objective to consume in everyone else's. In the first instance, for ethical consumption to be meaningful, consumers need more information in order to make ethical decisions. This is where Basu and Hicks (2008, p. 470) argue that 'social labels' come in, as they directly 'target the information distortion created by a lack of information regarding production methods'. However, not all products bear social labels and the related issues of informing and educating consumers remain a challenge. The multidimensionality of ethical consumption also complicates ethical decision-making. For those who are concerned with a cross-section of ethical concerns, there are 'problematic trade-offs between ethical bottom lines embedded in ethical products' (Low and Davenport, 2007, p. 341). Here Low and Davenport offer the example of choosing between foods produced locally with a low carbon footprint, compared to sourcing organic foods produced in developing countries (Low and Davenport, 2007, p. 341). This leads to a third problem – the way in which ethical consumption has been defined and by whom could also be considered problematic.

Low and Davenport (2007, p. 341) argue that 'the idea of being an ethical consumer as conceptualised [in wealthy countries] has little resonance with Southern consumers'. This raises the question: whose concerns does ethical consumption platform? Even while initiatives like Fairtrade focus on issues in developing countries, ethical consumption itself occurs in predominantly developed countries. It may be a luxury only afforded to consumers in affluent societies, whose needs have evolved beyond the 'basic needs' that concern consumers in poorer contexts (see Newholm and Shaw, 2007, p. 254). Even within wealthier economies, ethical consumption is perceived as the domain of a stratum of wealthy consumers: 'those able to spend the time, energy, and money to buy organic, drink fair trade, and invest ethically' (Barnett et al., 2005, p. 22). This raises the concern that not only wealthy countries but also wealthy consumers within are driving the ethical consumption agenda. Conversely it could be argued that greater incomes confer greater responsibility on affluent consumers to use their purchasing votes 'ethically' (see Dickinson and Carsky, 2005, p. 26). Whether they best represent the concerns of producers in often distant lands, these consumers are perhaps best placed, and arguably most obligated, to offer their solidarity.

Ethical consumption certainly stretches understanding of the importance of consumption and the responsibilities of consumers. Even so, the rationale of ethical consumption – while expanding traditional conceptions of the consumer – is still intrinsically tied to the logic of a market economy. Essentially ethical consumers aspire to exert influence on key issues through the market mechanism. For ethical consumption to be effective, there must be 'power in numbers'. There must also be a corresponding shift in the goods and services that are on offer. As such we could expect to see a rise in ethical consumption as well as a qualitative change in the goods and services that conventional businesses bring to the table.

The consumer: One dollar, one vote?

Frank A. Fetter (in Dickinson and Carsky, 2005, p. 25) provocatively puts forward that '[e]very buyer . . . determines in some degree the direction of industry. The market is a democracy where every penny gives the right to vote.' When the authority of national governments is disciplined through the relative authority of regional and global regulatory mechanisms, and when the power of states often gives way to the power of corporations, it is no surprise that domestic electoral votes might begin to pale in significance to the purchasing votes of everyday consumers, whereby the attention of elusive global actors is sought. It is in this broader context of the changing global, social, political and economic fabric that the role of consumption – in particular ethical consumption – rises in importance. This section revisits the construct of the 'consumer citizen' next to that of 'corporate citizen', by examining debates over the relative role, responsibilities and power of these two actors and how they connect and influence each other through ethical consumption practices.

The consumer citizen

The notion of the consumer citizen elevates the role of consumption beyond base monetary transaction to one with social and political dimensions (as discussed in the previous section). It also suggests, however, that consumers have a direct voice and that, armed with 'knowledge' of the impact of their purchases, have both the responsibility and the power to act. This indicates a level of compatibility between the concept of consumer citizenship and consumer sovereignty, where the latter suggests consumers 'may have enough power to institute desired changes' (Dickinson and Carsky, 2005, p. 28). Instead of simply signalling price and quality preferences, consumer sovereignty may instead be harnessed by ethical consumers to convey ethical preferences and accordingly effect meaningful change in the market (Dickinson and Carsky, 2005, p. 35). There is certainly evidence to support the rise of the consumer citizen.

There are a number of indications that everyday consumers have a sense of civic responsibility when it comes to economic transactions. Increasingly, polls delve into consumer attitudes with regard to ethical consumption. For example, Consumers International (CI, 2010) conducted a survey of 'consumer attitudes and awareness in relation to supermarkets and responsible trading practices' across six countries in Europe. When asked, 'How supermarkets should treat suppliers', respondents across Belgium (78 per cent), France (70 per cent), Denmark (70 per cent), Poland (65 per cent) and Spain (59 per cent) resoundingly supported that supermarkets 'pay enough to ensure good wages' (CI, 2010, p. 18). Only respondents in Greece favoured the alternative response, with 70 per cent favouring that supermarkets 'ensure lowest prices by paying minimum to suppliers' (CI, 2010, p. 18). Ipsos MORI (2009a), in an online survey of just over 23,000 people across 23 countries, found that on average, 77 per cent of respondents valued corporate social responsibility (CSR) as an 'important' factor in their purchasing decisions, compared to the 20 per cent that saw this as 'not important'. Yet consumer attitudes are not necessarily the best measure to predict purchasing behaviours.

The 'so-called attitude behaviour gap' drives increasing concern with attitude in theories of consumer decision-making (Newholm and Shaw, 2007, p. 256). Indeed, the phenomenon has been branded with numerous labels. It has also been referred to as the 'ethics gap' or '30:3' syndrome, where the latter refers to surveyed consumer preferences compared to poor rates of ethical purchases (Low and Davenport, 2007, p. 342). In a joint report by AccountAbility (AA) and the National Consumer Council (NCC), Forstater, Oelschaegel and Sillanpää (2006, p. 9) note that, for example, the preference of close to 90 per cent of people in the UK for free range eggs has only converted into 50 per cent sales. Likewise, while over 80 per cent of shoppers wish to reduce the carbon footprint associated with food sourcing, this has only converted into approximately one quarter of shoppers looking for the country of origin on food labels (Forstater, Oelschaegel and Sillanpää, 2006, p. 9). This raises many theories, including that perhaps the ethical consumer is simply a 'myth' (see Forstater, Oelschaegel and Sillanpää, 2006, p. 9). Or, perhaps, traditional and ethical product attributes compete, and base self-interest continues to trounce or undermine expressions of civic duty in consumption?

Many argue that traditional product attributes such as price and convenience continue to win favour with consumers over ethical attributes (see Low and Davenport, 2007, p. 342). Lang and Gabriel (2005, p. 53) point out that '[m]uch as we would like consumers to take the "high" road, evidence suggests that there are powerful forces pushing and pulling consumers in different and "low" roads too'. Ethical products, by definition, must cost more. They internalise costs, such as those related to the environment, which are typically externalised for conventional products (Lang and Gabriel, 2005, p. 53). Yet, despite concerns about the actualisation of ethical preferences in hard economic purchasing decisions, there is also strong evidence that ethical consumption is steadily on the rise.

The Cooperative Bank (2010) produced a study of a range of ethical markets in the UK. Comparing data for 2000 and 2010, it is clear that ethical consumption across a range of priority areas, including the environment (e.g. green cars), human rights (e.g. Fairtrade) and animal welfare (e.g. free range eggs), is on the rise. For example, organic purchases more than doubled in ten years, rising from £605 million in 2000 to £1527 million in 2010 (Cooperative Bank, 2010). In the same time period, the purchase of free-range eggs rose from £182 million to £483 million, green cars from £4 million to £846 million, ethical shareholdings from £4 million to £70 million and ethical cosmetics from £175 million to £528 million (Cooperative Bank, 2010). Fairtrade stands out among these as one of the ethical consumables which has experienced the highest growth levels. It rose from £33 million in 2000 to £1017 million in 2010 (Cooperative Bank, 2010). Importantly, the rise of these markets already indicates that there has been a significant shift towards ethical production to match consumer demand for such products. The very existence of such markets suggests that there has been a corporate response to ethical consumption already. However, it is not clear whether such small shifts can really lead to broader ethical transformation in consumption practices.

Impact on corporate behaviour

As we increasingly look to the ethical consumer to advance social agendas, equally we turn to the corporation to play its part. However, notions of responsibility attached to these two economic actors are arguably quite different, not least as corporations are more commonly profiled as the underlying 'problem', rather than the solution to ethical issues. Nevertheless ethical consumption aims specifically to signal a demand for ethical goods and services to the conventional businesses that source them in the market. As such initiatives like Fairtrade not only seek to connect producers and consumers but also to build meaningful connections between consumers and the corporate actors who mediate global exchange flows. However, it is unclear whether ethical consumers are having the desired impact on corporate behaviour.

While all manner and scale of conventional businesses face increasing pressure to act responsibly, not just with a view to their bottom line, corporations are particularly targeted due to their influence in the global market economy. Corporations are unique economic actors. They are defined not only by their scale of operations but also their loose connection to individual markets or countries. Increasingly global in their structure and scale of operations, many corporations' budgets dwarf those of whole governments. This becomes apparent when we compare data on the Gross National Income (GNI) of individual countries for 2010 (World Bank, 2011) to the revenues of the top global corporations for the same year (CNN Money, 2012). Table 8.1 shows that we would need to slot six corporations in among the top 40 income-earning countries for 2010 starting with Wal-Mart Stores, which ousts Austria in position 25. Of course, if we looked further down the line at lower income-earning countries, more corporations make an appearance. For example, there are eight corporations between Bangladesh (ranked 57) and Vietnam (ranked 58) (see World Bank, 2011; CNN Money, 2012). It is statistics like these, which have spurred debates over corporate regulation, including the existence of a perhaps de facto model of (ethical) consumer regulation.

Today, corporations operate in a highly deregulated economic environment. The process of trade liberalisation has progressively pulled back regulatory measures (see Chapter 3), but even without this it is difficult to envision how governments and even global regulatory measures might best work to regulate corporate behaviour, given the sheer scale of

Table 8.1 Top six global corporations in top 40 countries (2010)

Country (by rank) or corporation	GNI or revenue (million USD)
1. United States	14,600,828
2. China	5,700,018
3. Japan	5,369,116
4. Germany	3,537,180
5. France	2,749,821
+ 19 countries	*416,905+*
Wal-Mart Stores	**408,214**
25. Austria	391,511
26. Argentina	343,636
+ 6 countries	*286,676+*
Royal Dutch Shell	**285,129**
ExxonMobil	**284,650**
34. Colombia	255,290
35. Finland	252,958
BP	**246,138**
36. Portugal	232,590
+ 4 countries	*207,193+*
Toyota Motor	**204,106**
Japan Post Holdings	**202,196**

Sources: World Bank (2011); CNN Money (2012).

leading corporations. It is in this context that ethical consumers may in fact step in to fill the breach. Clouder and Harrison (2005, p. 102) note that 'ethical purchase behaviour is particularly useful at addressing global issues where national governments are reluctant to regulate'. While positive purchasing practices may be out of reach for poorer consumers, Clouder and Harrison (2005, p. 102) argue that boycotts are a viable mechanism for all. Certainly we have seen an uptake on consumer preferences through the rise of CSR.

Like the rise in ethical consumption, there is an arguably corresponding uptake of the CSR ethos in the corporate sector. There are some strong indications that this has been driven by the growing relevance of ethical consumption. Forstater, Oelschaegel and Sillanpää (2006, p. 21) argue that a key driver of corporate responsibility 'has been the realisation that beyond the emerging niche of active ethical consumers, mainstream consumers also want the brands that they put their trust in to come with environmental and social responsibility built in, not as added extra'. In this sense, both the increase of ethical consumption as discussed in previous sections and trends in consumer attitudes may be having an impact on corporate behaviour. For example, in the same report, Forstater, Oelschaegel and Sillanpää (2006, p. 21) cite a range of compelling statistics, including that 70 per cent of people in the UK in 2006 expressed an interest 'in learning about how companies are making an effort to behave responsibly', while 62 per cent said they were prepared to 'pay a premium for goods produced by responsible companies'. Statistics such as these are sending a clear message.

In a survey of 12,000 consumers in 2000, spanning 12 countries in Europe, it was found that 70 per cent of consumers factored a company's CSR commitments into their purchasing decisions, while 20 per cent claimed that they would pay more for products that were environmentally and socially responsible (CSR Europe, 2001, p. 10). CSR Europe (2001, p. 10), who commissioned the survey, concluded from such data that 'businesses have a clear opportunity to benefit by responding to ethical consumers'. Essentially, ethical consumption is increasingly seen as an essential consideration for companies seeking to protect their bottom line. Ipsos MORI (2009a, p. 1), based on surveys of ethical consumers across 23 countries, concluded that 'a small but influential group of consumers can have a disproportionate effect on the reputation and success of companies and brands'. These 'brand influencers', specifically the steady 43 per cent of consumers surveyed in 2007 and again in 2009, claim they factor CSR into their purchasing decisions (Ipsos MORI, 2009b, p. 2). Of particular interest is that almost 70 per cent claimed that in the past year (survey conducted April 2009) they had 'advised someone against a product, service or company' with two-thirds claiming 'that they have actually changed that person's mind about buying a product or service' (Ipsos Mori, 2009b, p. 1).

There may, however, be limitations to the level of 'transformation' we can read into ethical consumption and the corporate uptake on this. While there may be a shift towards CSR and ethical products and services, is this predominantly a matter of 'lip service' on the part of the corporate sector? Mayo (2005, p. xviii) argues that 'the discovery . . . [of ethical consumers] by commercial giants is also leading to shallow "ethics lite" products, stripped of their values and their transformative power, and with the potential to confuse consumers'. This suggests that there is the potential that the momentum generated by ethical consumers may be undermined by shallow corporate responses. Loureiro and Lotade (2005, p. 130) go so far as to suggest that corporations may simply be offering and promoting labels like Fair Trade 'to create a reputation for ethical behaviour in international trade practices'. This concern is taken up in the next section.

Fairtrade consumption: Corporate 'buy-in' or Fairtrade 'sell-out'?

This section problematises the participation of conventional businesses in Fairtrade labelling, for coffee. It poses the question whether corporate use of the label represents a buy-in to core Fairtrade values or not. This in turn has implications for how we might understand the effectiveness of consumer votes for Fairtrade. A consumer survey conducted by an ATO in the US in 2008 found that while 71.4 per cent of consumers had heard of Fair Trade, less than 6 per cent could name an ATO without assistance, and less than 10 per cent had made a recent purchase from an ATO (FTF, 2009, p. 17). Indeed, the analysis that ensues suggests that a deeper understanding of the ethical choices available in the Fair Trade sector itself, whereby consumers build a deeper understanding of Fairtrade offerings, is warranted. It also suggests that corporate uptake of the ethical consumer agenda may, in some cases, remain quite limited.

At the outset, it is important to acknowledge that Fairtrade labelling creates rules for business behaviour, specifically the terms of the relationship between business and producers, with regard to any products traded as Fairtrade. These 'rules of engagement' were examined in Chapter 5 and do indeed confer expectations upon participating businesses that exceed any requirements in the conventional market (which does not dictate the 'social responsibilities' of businesses or impose 'value distribution' requirements). Accordingly, any participating business, whether an ATO or a conventional business, is required to satisfy a number of requirements for the trade of any Fairtrade product, including paying minimum prices and premiums and offering pre-financing and/or credit. However, as an ATO critique of the participation of conventional businesses in Fairtrade indicates, there is a fundamental problem with this. Conventional businesses are only required to conform to these rules for that portion of their business dedicated to the trade in Fairtrade goods (which may be a very small portion indeed).

It is also important to gain an understanding of the type of conventional businesses that have joined the Fairtrade market. Many of them are small businesses, but they also include large corporate and often multinational enterprises, including Starbucks, Dunkin' Donuts, Green Mountain Coffee Roasters and Wal-Mart in the case of coffee (TransFair USA, n.d., p. 31). What opportunities has the corporate participation in Fairtrade offered smallholder coffee producers? We know that the engagement of conventional business has been crucial for mainstreaming the concept of Fairtrade, thereby providing access to conventional retail spaces. However, we also know that many conventional businesses have received boosts to their reputation by participating in Fairtrade, which TransFair USA recognised when it introduced the entry of conventional player Dunkin' Donuts into Fairtrade markets in 2003, observing that '[a] nationwide launch helped Dunkin' Donuts boost its reputation as an innovator in socially responsible business' (TransFair USA, 2004, p. 12).

The following evaluation of the participation of conventional businesses will raise the question of whether such a 'boost' to the reputation of conventional businesses like Dunkin' Donuts is really warranted. This problematises the discussion of ethical consumption thus far, as it may suggest that ethical consumption through Fairtrade is only having a very limited impact on corporate behaviour.

Are conventional companies 'free-riding' on Fairtrade?

Starbucks CEO, Howard Schultz (quoted in TransFair USA, n.d., p. 32), claims that the company is 'strongly committed to buying and serving responsibly grown and ethically traded coffee' and that 'TransFair USA has become a vital partner in this mission'. The question put forward by many ATOs is whether a strong commitment to marginalised growers and ethical trade is really demonstrated through a company's partnership with Fairtrade labelling for only a portion of its products. Dean's Beans (2010b), a coffee roasting cooperative/ATO estimates that there are 'less than a dozen of us 100% Fair Trade coffee companies in the USA' (i.e. 100 per cent fair trade activity, ATOs). Kornell (2007, 14) explains that there are many '100 percenters' in the US market, which are concerned that Fairtrade does not openly differentiate between the Fairtrade commitment of ATOs and conventional companies. Kornell (2007, p. 14) notes that the key concern raised by these ATOs is that 'the consequence of such a come-one, come-all approach [in Fairtrade labelling] is the dilution of the social justice mission at the core of the fair trade movement'. In many ways, the key concern is not so much whether conventional companies participate in Fairtrade, but how this impacts on the integrity of Fair Trade and its future.

Dean Cycon of Dean's Beans (Kornell, 2007, p. 14) claims that there is an additional consequence to the participation of conventional business in Fairtrade. He argues that 'if there's no differentiation between the 100 percenters and the dabblers' consumers are misled about the real commitment of the traders participating in Fairtrade, and that this will undermine 'the integrity of the label'. What consumers are not told is that conventional companies are not committed to Fairtrade principles for all of their trade activities; they are simply committed, argue Dean's Beans (2010b), to another 'product' that they can market to their consumer base with Fair Trade relegated to the work of 'marketing departments' and limited to 'just another offering' on the menu board. This raises the question: what are the conventional companies getting from participating in a labelling scheme, considering they only dedicate a small portion of their trade to Fairtrade activity?

It could be argued that by failing to be transparent on how 'Fairtrade' a company actually is, Fairtrade labelling, through its silence, overstates the commitment of conventional companies and gives them a largely undeserved PR boost. Tim Dominick of Sacred Grounds, another coffee ATO (Kornell, 2007, p. 14), explains that the low commitment of conventional companies does raise this question of their motivation, noting, for example, that 'Wal-Mart is doing fair trade now, and it is notorious for mistreating the workers'. So while Wal-Mart argues that '[w]e care deeply about the hard-working farmers who grow the products we sell', and that 'Fair Trade helps us to support a better living for those deserving farmers and their families' (Lee Scott, Chairman of the Executive Committee of the Board of Directors for Wal-Mart, quoted in TransFair USA, n.d., p. 34), this begs the question: why not step up its commitment to ethical trade practices? This in turn raises the concern that conventional companies may be using the device of the label, not to demonstrate a real commitment to Fairtrade principles, but to boost or repair their public image.

While many ATOs do recognise that conventional companies provide a means to reach a wider consumer base (Kornell, 2007, p. 14), they are concerned that Fairtrade does not differentiate between the commitment and practices of ATOs and conventional businesses. The significance is that while Fairtrade tries to battle the immiserating conditions in the conventional market, it does so by inviting conventional businesses (which effectively endorse the conventional market through most of their business activities) into its ranks.

The value of 'big business'

So what is it that conventional businesses offer that Fair Trade, through its mainstream strategies, primarily Fairtrade labelling but also branding (e.g. Cafédirect), is so keen to harness? It is access to the majority of consumers that makes getting the 'big boys' on side so appealing. If we look at the example of Starbucks, then even the minimal commitment of a corporation such as this can be immensely significant for the development of Fairtrade markets. Indeed, since Starbucks first began purchasing Fairtrade coffee in 2000 (Starbucks, 2010), its commitment to Fairtrade has continued to grow. In 2009 it purchased 39 million pounds of Fairtrade coffee (an increase of 20 million pounds compared to the previous year) and earned its place as the largest Fairtrade coffee purchaser in the world (Starbucks, 2010). Further, while its Fairtrade coffee purchases still only represented just over 10 per cent of total purchases (367 million pounds) in 2009, it sourced 81 per cent through its own ethical sourcing model – C.A.F.E. Practices (see Starbucks, 2010).[1] This suggests that ethical consumption may be on the rise through a mix of public and private initiatives, some more rigorous than others, than through singular models like Fairtrade.

Chapter 6 explored the parameters of the Fairtrade coffee market, observing that this remains a niche in the broader coffee market. However, if we examine trends across sustainability certifications generally, we can see that ethical consumption in coffee more generally has grown beyond the constraints of a market niche. This suggests that ethical labels like Fairtrade are beginning to reach a broader consumer base and with it a broader host of conventional market players. In a recent report produced for the International Trade Centre (ITC), Pierrot et al. (2010, p. 6) claim that '[c]ertified coffee is no longer a small market niche' with the estimate that in 2009, sustainability certifications applied to 8 per cent of the global trade in green coffee. While certified green coffee availability exceeds the volume traded (Pierrot Gio Vannucci and Kasterine, 2010, p. 4), sustainability certifications have certainly captured a very significant segment of the market. In terms of annual growth, certified coffee is also outperforming conventional coffee with an approximate average of 20–25 per cent annually compared to that of 2 per cent in the mainstream market (Pierrot, Giovannucci and Kasterine, 2010, p. 13). Then in individual markets, certified coffees have captured 40 per cent of the Dutch market; 16 per cent of the US market; and 10 per cent of those for Denmark, Sweden and Norway (Pierrot, Gio Vannucci and Kasterine, 2010, p. 4). The certifications considered in preparing this data were Fairtrade, Organic, Utz Certified, Rainforest Alliance and the Common Code for the Coffee Community (4C) (see Pierrot, Gio Vannucci and Kasterine, 2010, p. 4). This diversity in labels, though, also signals one of the difficulties consumers face in making ethical purchases. Understanding the different ethical agendas and deliverables is difficult as demonstrated in the previous discussion. For example, of these certifications, only Fairtrade offers a price floor and premium for participating producers (Pierrot, Gio Vannucci and Kasterine, 2010, pp. 6–7). This begs the question: do consumers understand the ethical choices available to them, and therefore the significance of their ethical purchases?

Conclusion

Low and Davenport (2007, p. 339) argue that 'shopping for a better world' does not challenge the prevailing market logic, and as such does not hold the answer to the broader social and political transformations needed. It is of course appealing to both consumers and corporations alike that consumers might 'painlessly and almost effortlessly create social and political change' through their consumption practices (Low and Davenport, 2007, p. 339). Yet Low and Davenport (2007, p. 340) suggest the formula might be just a little too easy, allowing consumers to 'shop for a better world from the comfort of their armchairs through the convenience of the Internet, without having to engage with time-consuming campaigns – social transformation can be easy, clean and fun!' Indeed, while consumers express a commitment to ethical purchasing, it is not clear that they fully understand the ethical choices available and the impact of their support of particular strategies. It is also not clear that ethical consumption is creating a deep change in corporate behaviour. This may lend support to Low and Davenport's (2007, p. 346) argument that the time has come to 're-politicise ethical consumption'.

9
Conclusion

A poignant quote from a cooperative leader in Papua New Guinea captures the impact of low coffee incomes (especially where they fail to cover even the costs of production), on the smallholder coffee producers in his village: 'If we don't get enough [money] we won't work hard; it will demoralise us' (Cooperative Leader A, 2004). This message has been heard, it has been embraced, and it has been acted on through the development of the Fairtrade label, offering a 'better deal' for marginalised producers. Initiatives like Fairtrade demonstrate that another crucial point has been understood. Marginalised producers like this may *feel demoralised* but it is the consumers – be it the traders, retailers or individual end consumers – that *should* feel demoralised. Allowing and thereby effectively condoning an unequal exchange such as that which characterises the conventional coffee trade to occur and, even worse, to continue is, after all, inexcusable. The responsibility of traders and consumers has been grasped within Fair Trade networks, but what remedies does the Fairtrade label really offer marginalised producers in the developing world? This depends of course on which producers are examined: the minority supplying the Fairtrade market or the majority who are excluded?

The case of coffee has been examined in this book. Fairtrade in coffee is a vibrant market, which offers unique opportunities for smallholder coffee producers. There is a catch, however; this vibrant market only occupies a niche of the conventional market, leaving the bulk of smallholder producers still supplying their coffee through conventional channels. Certainly Fairtrade coffee offers a whole range of opportunities for the smallholder producers that are able to gain certification. In integrated alternative trade networks, the activities of the ATOs and NGOs that endeavour to support marginalised producers in a range of commodities, create significant opportunities for the lucky few producer organisations that participate. With the advent of Fairtrade labelling, access to conventional retail spaces also emerged through the participation of conventional businesses that satisfy Fairtrade product standards. Indeed, the Fair Trade movement generally, and Fairtrade in coffee in particular, set a precedent that justifiably challenges the performance of free trade in coffee. Fairtrade does not presently, however, offer opportunities to the bulk of smallholder coffee producers, *who need to be reached.*

The crisis at the turn of the twenty-first century demonstrates the urgency for trade reform in the conventional coffee market, through which opportunities could be extended to the bulk of smallholder coffee producers. The livelihoods of some 25 million growers, their families and their communities who rely on coffee income for food, health, education and infrastructure investments were undermined as quickly and as severely as the prices plunged. Coffee, which is grown predominantly in developing countries, spelled a developmental disaster. While the previous regulatory regime in coffee was plagued with problems that ultimately sealed its demise, it nonetheless sets the subsequent poor performance of free trade in coffee in a dismal light. There has always been volatility in coffee prices, largely due to volatility in supply (which often hinges on natural occurrences such as frost). But the depth of crisis through price collapse and the squeeze on value retained in coffee-producing countries, both for growers and for exporters, escalated as quickly as trade liberalisation in coffee was phased in. The immiseration that came with it underscores the importance of ensuring that there is also meaningful reform in the conventional trade sector, alongside reforms already undertaken in the Fairtrade niche.

Nevertheless, arguably by endorsing 'part-time Fairtraders' like Procter & Gamble and Starbucks, who conduct the bulk of their trade activities in the conventional market, Fairtrade is not in the best position to push for far-reaching change in conventional business practices. The strength of the Fairtrade model lies in its capacity to mainstream Fairtrade products; yet isn't Fair Trade or Fairtrade about changing trade relationships? This is certainly the view taken by an ATO, critical of the implications of how conventional businesses participate in Fairtrade, with Dean's Beans (2010a) arguing that '[i]t's important to remember that Fair Trade is an economic agreement, it's not a type of coffee'. While most commercial businesses and consumers view, or at least access, Fairtrade coffee as just another differentiated coffee product, alongside mocha and cappuccino, it is unlikely that the Fairtrade model can provide the basis for the broader change needed to lift millions of smallholder coffee producers, not just a few, out of poverty.

The limitations of the Fairtrade development model

Since its first introduction into the Dutch coffee market in the late 1980s, the Fairtrade model has arguably revolutionised the way we think about both trade and aid. It does this by employing a combined 'trade and aid' development strategy, working towards a meaningful interface between the two. It moves beyond traditional non-governmental aid models by stepping in from the sidelines, getting active in the business of trade, and thereby seeking to empower producers by carving out and providing them access to fairer economic opportunities within the conventional market, controversially enlisting the help of conventional businesses. However, its empowerment through trade philosophy is also tempered by the requirement of a Fairtrade premium, which is essentially an aid payment. Here too, however, Fairtrade is different. It has built an aid transfer into its trading terms, ensuring that these monies come from the trading partners that Fairtrade producer's supply. While Fairtrade has pioneered a unique approach, the legitimacy of this approach, nonetheless, is in question.

First, the trade and aid elements of the Fairtrade model clash. If the intention is to empower producers through trade by providing them with trading opportunities that are equitable and incomes that can support their needs, then why the requirement for an aid payment? Second, the critique of conventional trade underpinning the Fairtrade strategy is at odds with the practices it has developed. If conventional trade is 'unfair', why work within the system at all? Why enlist the participation of conventional businesses that will only service Fairtrade terms 'part-time' (for Fairtrade products) and not for the bulk of their activities?

It is clear that Fairtrade is aiming to create an applied critique of the conventional market – an alternative from within – which aims to model 'fairer' trade practices. However, in so doing, it also provides consumers and businesses with a time-out from the main game or an ethical outlet into which they can channel their ethical inclinations, if you will. Even so, the Fairtrade niche which consumers are pouring their energies into does not reform the structure of the global trading system or regulate reform of conventional businesses. To borrow an economic term, it may create an 'opportunity cost', considering that perhaps such energies could more effectively be directed at strategies seeking broader trade reform.

Fairtrade: Moving forward

> My major argument about Fairtrade is that it provides an excuse avenue for people not to tackle the difficult issues, the difficult questions: 'Coffee crisis? We drink Fairtrade coffee – problem solved – we don't have to do anymore, we've done the action, we've bought the Fairtrade'.
>
> Mick Wheeler, Specialty Coffee Association of Europe

It may be unrealistic to expect Fairtrade to rival the authority of the conventional market. However, while it does not have the capacity to transform the conventional market, it is important that it does not redirect the energies of 'consumer citizens' from other campaign strategies for market reform. As Fairtrade remains a niche market, two possible scenarios present themselves. The first possibility is that Fairtrade is indeed diverting attention away from more meaningful market-reforming efforts and may even be reinforcing the legitimacy of conventional businesses as it boosts their reputation. The second possibility is that Fairtrade is fostering increased awareness of global trade inequities by educating and recruiting ethical consumers, which helps to build a groundswell of demand for greater trade reform in the future.

The main chapters in this book would appear to support the first scenario. While Fairtrade has had a positive impact on participating producers, and while it also models an 'ideal' of better trading terms, key reforms in the conventional market are still needed. Further energy on achieving broader trade reforms, is thus warranted. However, the final chapter in this book provided a preliminary examination of the broader 'ethical consumption' phenomenon to which Fairtrade belongs. Here we can see that the second scenario may actually have some promise. While there may be challenges for (ethical) consumers to understand the range of ethical choices available to them, and to ensure they make appropriate purchasing 'votes', ethical consumption has certainly gathered strong momentum. Indeed, in the coffee sector, sustainable sourcing certifications, including Fairtrade, have grown to capture almost 10 per cent of the coffee trade. The challenge for Fairtrade moving forward is to work towards the realisation of this second scenario.

Notes

1 Introduction

1. The terminology of 'south' and 'developing' and 'north' and 'developed' are used interchangeably.

2 What's Fair about Fair Trade

1. For a short history of the campaign for a social clause, see Sukthankar and Nova (2004).

3 The Market: An Unequal Exchange?

1. Agricultural supports as a percentage of the gross value of farm receipts fell from a 37 per cent average in 1986–8 to a 30 per cent average in 2003–5 (World Bank, 2007, p. 97).
2. Here Polaski (2007, p. 4) refers to the arguments made by a group of developing countries, which have joined together as the Group of 33 or 'G33'.
3. For example, in the 1983 agreement, the 'agreed' range was 120–40 US cents/lb (ICO, 2007a).
4. Raw harvested coffee is called 'cherry' and must be processed to parchment within 24 hours if the quality of the bean is to be maintained. Thus, processing attracts additional value due to the additional labour input, and also the improved quality of the bean as producers can now ensure it is processed in time before it is sold on.

4 The Birth of a Movement and Trade Alternative

1. Note: There are clear exceptions as discussion of alternative trade models reaches beyond Fair Trade strategies to include initiatives like organics, for example. The relevance of the alternative trade label is examined in this chapter due to the origins of Fair Trade in the activities of ATOs.
2. Today, the WFTO is the international association for ATOs/FTOs. It has undergone two name changes since its creation as the International Federation for Alternative Trade in 1991: first it was renamed the International Fair Trade Association and more recently (in 2009) it was renamed the World Fair Trade Organisation (WFTO).
3. While uncommon, some authors still refer to ATOs (for example, see Riedl, 2009 and Shreck, 2005).
4. The membership comprises stakeholders from production to consumption in alternative trade networks, including producer cooperatives and associations, export marketing companies, importers, retailers, national and regional Fair Trade networks and financial institutions, dedicated to Fair Trade principles.

The WFTO comprises over 450 organisations spanning 75 countries across Africa, Asia, Europe, Latin America, and the North American and Pacific Rim (WFTO, 2012a). Regional producer networks represented in this international body include the WFTO Asia, Cooperation for Fair Trade in Africa (COFTA), WFTO Latin America, WFTO Pacific Rim and WFTO Europe (WFTO, 2012a). WFTO membership also includes the European Fair Trade Association (EFTA) and the Fair Trade Federation (FTF – based in the Americas), as well as a host of national networks.

5. Note: the WFTO also has responsibilities for market development and advocacy (WFTO, 2012b)
6. Note: ATOs that seek to become members of the WFTO are assessed through a three-step accreditation process comprising: (1) 'Self-Assessment Reports' (SAR) – which require the applicant to self-assess its conformity to WFTO principles, by completing a WFTO form and providing documentary evidence to support its claims; (2) 'Review and Feedback' – here the WFTOs monitoring department reviews SAR and provides feedback with the aim to enable applicants to improve their understanding of WFTO principles (and therefore compliance to these) in the future; (3) 'Approval' – where external readers score applicants against WFTO standards with a minimum score required for approval to be granted (WFTO, 2009). Where there are 'complaints or to resolve other issues regarding the SAR', a fourth step – 'External Verification' – applies, whereby third-party verification of SARs is requested (WFTO, 2009).
7. Estimates draw on data for financial year 2006, except for data from ETHIQUABLE, AlterEco & Twin Trading, which refers to financial year 2004.
8. These are Equal Exchange (US), Ten Thousand Villages (US), and Alter Trade Japan with estimates based on data for financial year 2006 except data from Alter Trade Japan, which is financial year 2004.
9. Historically, Oxfam Fair Trade provides an important case study, but it withdrew from direct importing in the 1990s (in order to focus on campaigning and lobbying activities) (Krier, 2008, p. 103), now sourcing from other ATOs to supply its stores (Nicholls and Opal, 2005, p. 100).

5   Fairtrade: Peeling Back the Label

1. Product information on a packet of Jasper Fairtrade Coffee, Fairtrade and Organic Certified, purchased at Oxfam Shop, Broadway, Sydney, Australia in 2006.
2. Fairtrade Labelling Organisations International, the International Fair Trade Association, the Network of European Worldshops! and the European Fair Trade Association.
3. Carol Wills was the Executive Director of the WFTO, 1997–2005.
4. Now generally known by the shorthand Fairtrade International.
5. These networks are Coordinadora Lationamericana y del Caribe de Comercio Justo, Network of Asian Producers and Fairtrade Africa respectively.
6. FLO will be used to refer to the FLO superstructure, comprising FLO e.V, while FLO e.V will be used when referring specifically to this standard-setting body. It is important to note, however, that a separate Standards

Committee (which forms part of the FLO superstructure), works with FLO e.V and holds authority over it with regard to standard-setting.

7. Note: FLO-Cert also has its own internal Board of Directors in addition to answering to a shared Board of Directors with FLO e.V.

8. It is worth noting that all members of the Board are elected by the Annual General Assembly comprising equal representation of LIs and producers (FLO, 2011a).

9. In the case of minor changes to a standard, the SU Director can authorise these without referring them for approval to the SC (FLO Standards Unit, 2012a, p. 9).

10. A generic standard for Contract Production is also available to support the efforts of small-scale producers to organise and graduate to the generic standards for small-scale production (i.e. small-scale producers who in partnership with an organisation are in the process of forming an independent democratic organisational structure) (FLO, 2011g, p. 4). The scope of this standard is limited exclusively to new and already registered producers of Basmati rice and cotton in India and of cotton in Pakistan, as well as already registered producers of dried fruit in Pakistan (FLO, 2011g, p. 4). As such it will not be considered here, as it does not apply extensively across the Fairtrade producer base and not to coffee producers in particular.

11. Nevertheless, as will be shown in the following two sections, provisions are made for the treatment and welfare of hired labour, in the event that hired labour is employed by smallholder growers.

12. Note: Fairtrade standards are updated regularly. The current version of the Coffee Standard is dated 1 April 2011 and replaces the former version dated 16 February 2009 (FLO, 2011i). The current versions of the Producer Standard and the Trader Standard are dated 1 May 2011 and replace previous versions dated 15 August 2009 (FLO 2011j, 2011k).

13. Processing systems for coffee vary by the level of hulling of the coffee bean, as well as the process for doing this. This has implications for the classification of coffee for international trade where the washed system produces mild coffees; the natural system produces sun-dried or unwashed coffees; and the pulped natural system produces semi-washed, semi-dried or unwashed coffee (FLO, 2009c).

14. In green bean form, coffee has only been subject to minimal processing to optimise quality during storage and shipping.

6   Fairtrade Coffee: A Niche Market

1. As these figures are based on survey responses from 869 out of a total of 906 participating Fairtrade producer organisations, FLO estimates that there are likely 1.15 million participating producers (FLO, 2011o, p. 17).

2. Growers in Africa typically cultivate plots less than one hectare in size, compared to growers in Latin American origins that 'typically run farms that are five to ten times as big' (FLO, 2007c, p. 23).

3. Fairtrade also has standards for contract production and hired labour; though coffee is predominantly produced by smallholder growers' organisations and as such, these standards will be examined.

4. Current priority applications include banana, organic juice, orange juice, sugar and cotton producers (all origins), as well as a range of other products from specific origins (FLO, 2007d, pp. 2–3). These priorities likely reflect demand for new products and origins, or shortages in supply for existing products and origins. Coffee producers are currently not on the list of priority products.

7   Fairtrade Impacts on Coffee Producers

1. A Jasper Fairtrade Coffee, Fairtrade and Organic Certified, purchased at Oxfam Shop, Broadway, Sydney in 2006.
2. The additional premium for organics under the original pricing structure actually formed a part of the minimum price for double-certified coffee, raising the minimum price of double-certified coffee by US$ 0.15 per pound. Rather than maintaining a separate premium level for double-certified coffee, the 2007 version of the Coffee Standard makes provisions for buyers to 'pay a minimum organic differential' and this must be at least US$ 0.20 per pound (FLO, 2007e, p. 4). This new 'organic differential' replaced the old 'additional premium' for organics, serving as an additional payment that, like its predecessor, is added to the minimum price and not to the premium. Essentially this raised the Fairtrade minimum price for double-certified coffee by US$ 0.05 per pound.
3. 'Naturals' refers to unwashed Arabica.
4. Beyond the international representation provided by the ICA, cooperatives are also organised into sectoral associations. For agriculture, this is the International Cooperative Agricultural Organisation (ICAO) (ICA, 2006).
5. The OCS was established in April 2003 (OCS, n.d.) and replaces the previous 'Cooperative Societies Unit' (CSU).
6. All practice subsistence farming as well, and some also have additional sources of income (though coffee is the primary source of income for all).
7. Communal plots are not necessary; the cooperative model also facilitates joint marketing of the produce of individual plots.
8. Referring to Dean Cycon of 'Dean's Beans'.

8   Ethical Consumption: Revolution from Within?

1. In addition to purchasing Fairtrade-certified coffee, the company also sees its own sourcing strategies as an important part of its role in building 'stable relationships with farmers' (Starbucks, 2006). Starbucks (2005), in collaboration with Conservation International, developed its 'Coffee and Farmer Equity Practices' or 'C.A.F.E. Practices' programme in 2001. Suppliers must meet base standards to qualify as a Starbucks-preferred supplier, and in addition are rewarded if their performance stands out (Starbucks, 2005). With standards in the areas of 'product quality, economic accountability (transparency), social responsibility, environmental leadership in coffee growing and environmental leadership in coffee processing' (Starbucks, 2005), the company clearly attempts to serve both its economic interests as well as its perceived CSR commitments.

References

Ame, Henry T. (2006) Interview, General Manager, Coffee Connections, Coffee Connections Office, 13 December, Coffee Connections Offices, Goroka, Papua New Guinea.

Anderson, Tim and Elisabeth Riedl (2006) 'Fair Trade: The Scope of the Debate', *Australian Journal of Professional and Applied Ethics* (Special issue: *Global Justice and Global Prosperity*, Selected Papers from the Third ISBEE World Congress 2004), 8, 1, pp. 6–20.

Bagwell, Kyle and Robert W. Staiger (2001) 'Domestic Policies, National Sovereignty, and International Economic Institutions', *The Quarterly Journal of Economics*, May, pp. 519–62.

Barfield, Claude and Douglas Irwin (1997) 'The Future of Free Trade', *Business Economics*, April, pp. 26–31.

Barnett, Clive, Philip Cafaro and Terry Newholm (2005) 'Philosophy and Ethical Consumption', in Rob Harrison, Terry Newholm and Deirdre Shaw (eds), *The Ethical Consumer* (London: Sage Publications), pp. 11–24.

Barratt Brown, Michael (1993) *Fair Trade: Reform and Realities in the International Trading System* (London: Zed Books).

Basu, Arnab K. and Robert L. Hicks (2008) 'Label Performance and the Willingness to Pay for Fair Trade Coffee: A Cross-National Perspective', *International Consumer Studies*, 32, 5, pp. 470–78.

Bello, Walden (2005) *Dilemmas of Domination: The Unmaking of the American Empire* (New York: Metropolitan Books).

Bhagwati, Jagdish (1995) 'Trade Liberalisation and "Fair Trade" Demands: Addressing the Environmental and Labour Standards Issues', *World Economy*, 18, 6 pp. 745–59.

Bhagwati, Jagdish (1996) 'Introduction', in Jagdish Bhagwati and Robert E. Hudec (eds), *Fair Trade and Harmonization: Economic Analysis*, Vol. 1 (Cambridge, MA: MIT Press), pp. 1–6.

Bhagwati, Jagdish and Robert E. Hudec (eds) (1996a) *Fair Trade and Harmonization: Economic Analysis*, Vol. 1 (Cambridge, MA: MIT Press).

Bhagwati, Jagdish and Robert E. Hudec (eds) (1996b) *Fair Trade and Harmonisation: Legal Analysis*, Vol. 2 (Cambridge, MA: MIT Press).

Boonman, Mark, Wendela Huisman, Elmy Sarrucco-Fedorovtsjev and Terya Sarrucco (2011) *Fair Trade Facts & Figures: A Success Story for Producers and Consumers* (DAWS), http://www.european-fair-trade-association.org/efta/Doc/FT-E-2010.pdf, accessed on 28 May 2012.

Buckman, Greg (2005) *Past Mistakes, Future Choices* (London: Zed Books).

Byers, Elizabeth and Dean Cycon (2004) *Inter-Regional Case Study: Promoting Fair Trade Organic Mountain Coffee*, www.mountainpartnership.org/initiatives/products/Inter-regionalCaseStudy.pdf, accessed on 9 August 2007.

Cafédirect (2005) *Company History*, http://www.cafedirect.co.uk/about/company.php, accessed on 16 May 2005.

Cafédirect (2006) 'The Fair Trade Initiative: Sustainable Commercial Opportunity or Development Trap', Paper contributed for ITC Executive Forum on National Export Strategies – *Bringing the Poor into the Export Process: Linkages and Strategic Implications*, http://www.google.com.au/url?sa=t&rct=j&q=&esrc=s&source=w eb&cd=1&ved=0CCYQFjAA&url=http%3A%2F%2Fwww.intracen.org%2FWor kArea%2FDownloadAsset.aspx%3Fid%3D51813&ei=tJ-LUIHYEsqaiAegGg&us g=AFQjCNEeEa8LWx2cR8DDmYV1GCd7DOCGaQ&cad=rja, accessed on 27 October 2012.

Cafédirect (2008a) *Cafédirect PLC: Report and Financial Statement*, http://www.cafedirect.co.uk/ourbusiness/investorrelations/annualreports/, accessed on 8 April 2010.

Cafédirect (2008b) *The Gold Standards: Cafédirect Annual Report 2007–08*, http://www.cafedirect.co.uk/ourbusiness/investorrelations/annualreports/, accessed on 8 April 2010.

Cafédirect (2010a) *Cafédirect: The History*, http://www.cafedirect.co.uk/about_us/history/, accessed on 28 March 2010.

Cafédirect (2010b) *Our Business*, http://www.cafedirect.co.uk/our_business/. accessed on 28 March 2010.

Cafédirect (2010c) *Living up to Our Gold Standard in Challenging Times: Annual Report 2010*, www.cafedirect.co.uk/discover-our-difference/our-beliefs-2/, accessed on 23 October 2012.

Cafédirect (2011a) *Committed to Our Gold Standard: Annual Review 2011*, www.cafedirect.co.uk/discover-our-difference/our-beliefs-2/shareholders/, accessed on 20 October 2012.

Cafédirect (2011b) *Cafédirectplc: Report and Financial statements 31 December 2011*, www.cafedirect.co.uk/discover-our-difference/our-beliefs-2/shareholders/, accessed on 20 October 2012.

Clouder, Scott and Rob Harrison (2005) 'The Effectiveness of Ethical Consumer Behaviour', in Rob Harrison, Terry Newholm and Deirdre Shaw (eds), *The Ethical Consumer* (London: Sage Publications), pp. 89–104.

CNN Money (2012) Global 500, 26 July 2010 issue, http://money.cnn.com/magazines/fortune/global500/2010/full_list/index.html, accessed on 28 May 2012.

COFTA (2006) *Who we are*, http://catgen.com/cofta/EN/whoweare.html, accessed on 6 August 2007.

COFTA (2012a) *Introduction*, http://www.cofta.org/en/en/index.asp, accessed on 28 October 2012.

COFTA (2012b) *COFTA Members: View Members Listing*, http://www.cofta.org/en/en/members_listing.asp, accessed on 28 October 2012.

COFTA (2012c) *Country Networks*, http://www.cofta.org/en/en/countrynetworks. asp, accessed on 28 October 2012.

Consumers International and the International Institute for Environment and Development (2005) *From Bean to Cup: How Consumer Choice Impacts upon Coffee Producers and the Environment*, http://www.consumersinternational. org/news-and-media/publications/from-bean-to-cup-how-consumer-choice-impacts-upon-coffee-producers-and-the-environment, accessed on 27 October 2012.

Consumers International (2010) *Checked Out: Are European Supermarkets Living Up to their Responsibilities for Labour Conditions in the Developing World?*

March, London, http://www.consumersinternational.org/news-and-media/ publications, accessed on 5 May 2012.

Cooperative Bank (2010) *Ethical Consumerism Report 2011*, http://www.co-operative.coop/corporate/Investors/Publications/Ethical-Consumerism-Report/, accessed on 29 May 2012.

Cooperative Coffees (2010) *Welcome to Cooperative Coffees*, http://www.coopcoffees.com/, accessed on 22 May 2010.

Cooperative Leader A (2004) Interview, Growers Cooperative A, 7 December, Papua New Guinea.

Cooperative Leader B (2004) Interview, Growers Cooperative B, 8 December, Papua New Guinea.

Cooperative Societies Unit/Ministry of Trade and Industry (n.d.) *Cooperative Societies Unit of Papua New Guinea: Information Pamphlet*, Boroko, Papua New Guinea (obtained in-country in December 2004).

CSR Europe (2001) *CSR Europe Magazine*, January, http://www.csreurope.org/data/files/csr_magazine_january_2001.pdf, accessed on 26 May 2012.

Daviron, Benoit and Stefano Ponte (2005) *The Coffee Paradox: Global Markets, Commodity Trade and the Elusive Promise of Development* (London: Zed Books).

Dean's Beans (2010a) *Our New Profit Sharing Program – More Cash in the Hands of Farmers*, www.deansbeans.com/coffee/deans_zine.html?blogid=324, accessed on 8 April 2010.

Dean's Beans (2010b) *Fair Trade Roadmap*, http://www.deansbeans.com/coffee/fair_trade_roadmap.html, accessed on 4 May 2010.

Develtere, Patrick and Ignace Pollet (2005) *Cooperatives and Fair Trade*, Background paper commissioned by the Committee for the Promotion and Advancement of Cooperatives (COPAC) for the COPAC Open Forum on Fair Trade and Cooperatives, Berlin, February, http://www.copac.coop/about/2005/cooperatives-and-fair-trade-final.pdf, accessed on 28 May 2012.

Dickinson, Roger A. and Mary L. Carsky (2005) 'The Consumer as Economic Voter', in Rob Harrison, Terry Newholm and Deirdre Shaw (eds), *The Ethical Consumer* (London: Sage Publications), pp. 25–36.

Dunkley, Graham (2000) *The Free Trade Adventure: The WTO, the Uruguay Round and Globalism – A Critique* (London: Zed Books).

Eshuis, Fenny and Jos Harmsen (2003) *Making Trade Work for the Producers: 15 Years of Fairtrade Labelled Coffee in the Netherlands*, the Max Havelaar Foundation, November, the Netherlands, www.fairtrade.org.uk/downloads/pdf/making_trade_work.pdf, accessed on 6 March 2007.

Esteva, Gustavo (1992) 'Development', in Wolfgang Sachs (ed.), *The Development Dictionary: A Guide to Knowledge as Power* (London: Zed Books), pp. 6–25.

ETI (2012a) *About ETI*, http://www.ethicaltrade.org/about-eti, accessed on 28 October 2012.

ETI (2012b) *ETI Base Code*, http://www.ethicaltrade.org/eti-base-code, accessed on 28 October 2012.

Fair Trade USA (2011) *Almanac*, http://www.fairtradeusa.org/resource-library/downloads, accessed on 25 May 2012.

Fair Trade USA and FLO (2011) *Fair Trade USA Resigns Fairtrade International (FLO) Membership: Joint Statement*, 9/15/2011, http://www.fairtradeusa.org/print/node/49022, accessed on 22 May 2012.

Fairtrade Foundation (2006) *The History of Fairtrade Labelling*, http://www.fairtrade.org.uk/about_fairtrade_worldwide.htm, accessed on 7 February 2006.

Fair Trade Federation (2009) *Report on Trends in the North American Fair Trade Market*, March, http://fairtradefederation.org/ht/d/sp/i/271/pid/271, accessed on 30 May 2012.

FAO (2009) *The Market for Organic and Fair-Trade Coffee: Study Prepared in the Framework of FAO Project GCP/RAF/404/GER*, http://www.fao.org/fileadmin/templates/organicexports/docs/Market_Organic_FT_Coffee.pdf, accessed on 19 March 2010.

Fitter, Robert and Raphael Kaplinsky (2001) 'Who Gains from Product Rents as the Coffee Market becomes more Differentiated? A Value Chain Analysis', *Bulletin Paper*, Institute of Development Studies, May.

FLO (2003) *Annex A. A Quantum Leap in the Impact of Fairtrade Labelling: FLO's Strategic Plan 2003–2008*, December, http://www.fairtrade.net/uploads/media/Annex_A_Summary_of_FLO_Strategic_Plan.pdf, accessed on 12 July 2007.

FLO (2005) *Delivering Opportunities: Annual Report 2004/2005*, http://www.fairtrade.net/uploads/media/FLO_AR_2004_05.pdf, accessed on 18 January 2007.

FLO (2006a) *Liaison Officers*, http://www.fairtrade.net/liaison_officers.html, accessed on 13 July 2007.

FLO (2006b) *Coffee*, www.fairtrade.net/coffee.html, accessed 5 October 2007.

FLO (2007a) *The Producer Networks become Co-owners of FLO*, 22 June, http://www.fairtrade.net/single_view.html&cHash=53bdba3599&tx_ttnews[backPid]=104&tx_ttnews[tt_news]=20, accessed on 26 June 2007.

FLO (2007b) *An Inspiration for Change: Annual Report 2007*, http://www.fairtrade.net/annual_reports08.html, accessed on 10 March 2010.

FLO (2007c) *The Benefits of Fairtrade: A Monitoring and Evaluation Report of Fairtrade Certified Producer Organisations for 2007*, http://www.fairtrade.net/impact_studies.html, accessed on 10 March 2010.

FLO (2007d) *Producer Certification Fund: Guidelines* (September), http://www.fairtrade.net/producer_certification_fund.html, accessed on 10 March 2010.

FLO (2007e) *Fairtrade Standards for Coffee for Small Farmers' Organisations*, March, www.fairtrade.net/fileadmin/user_upload/content/Coffee_SF_March_2007_EN.pdf, accessed on 15 May 2007.

FLO (2008) *FLO Newsletter – February 2008*, http://www.fairtrade.net/333.html: accessed on 29 March 2010.

FLO (2009a) *Making a Difference: A New Global Strategy for Fairtrade, Fairtrade Labelling's Strategic Review (2007/2008)*, FTL Strategic Review Summary, March, http://www.fairtrade.net/our_new_strategy.html, accessed on 10 March 2010.

FLO (2009b) *Producer Services Relations Unit*, http://www.fairtrade.net/services_and_relations.html, accessed on 10 March 2010.

FLO (2009c) *Fairtrade Standards for Coffee for Small Producers' Organisations*, Version 16.2.2009, http://www.fairtrade.net/product_standards_smallproducers.html, accessed on 10 March 2010.

FLO (2009d) *Generic Fairtrade Trade Standards*, Version 15.08.2009, http://www.fairtrade.net/generic_trade_standards.html, accessed on 10 March 2010.

FLO (2010a) *Explanatory Document for the Generic Fairtrade Standard for Small Producers' Organisations*, January, http://www.fairtrade.net/654.html, accessed on 10 March 2010.

FLO (2010b) *Fairtrade Minimum Price and Fairtrade Premium Table*, Version 10.02.2010, www.fairtrade.net/generic_standars.html#c4426, accessed on 10 March 2010.

FLO (2011a) *How We're Run*, http://www.fairtrade.net/how_we_are_run.html, accessed on 16 March 2012.

FLO (2011b) *Board Members*, http://www.fairtrade.net/773.html, accessed on 16 March 2012.

FLO (2011c) *FLO Leadership Team*, http://www.fairtrade.net/970.html, accessed on 16 March 2012.

FLO (2011d) *Terms of Reference: FLO Standards Committee*, April, http://www.fairtrade.net/setting_the_standards.html, accessed on 11 April 2012.

FLO (2011e) *Liaison Officers*, http://www.fairtrade.net/liaison_officers.html, accessed on 11 April 2012.

FLO (2011f) *Producer Services and Relations Unit*, http://www.fairtrade.net/services_and_relations.html, accessed on 11 April 2012.

FLO (2011g) *Fairtrade Standard for Contract Production*, Version 1/5/2011, http://www.fairtrade.net/943.html, accessed on 21 May 2012.

FLO (2011h) *Aims of Fairtrade Standards*, http://www.fairtrade.net/aims_of_fairtrade_standards.html, accessed on 21 May 2012.

FLO (2011i) *Fairtrade Standard for Coffee for Small Producer Organisations*, Version 1/4/2011, http://www.fairtrade.net/our_standards.html, accessed on 19 May 2012.

FLO (2011j) *Fairtrade Standard for Small Producer Organisations*, Version 1/5/2011, http://www.fairtrade.net/our_standards.html, accessed on 19 May 2012.

FLO (2011k) *Generic Fairtrade Trade Standard*, Version 1/5/2011, http://www.fairtrade.net/our_standards.html, accessed on 19 May 2012.

FLO (2011l) *Product Standards for Small Producer Organisations*, http://www.fairtrade.net/product_standards_smallproducers.html, accessed on 21 May 2012.

FLO (2011m) *Product Standards for Hired Labour*, http://www.fairtrade.net/product_standards_hiredlabour0.html, accessed on 21 May 2012.

FLO (2011n) *Q&A on Fairtrade International and Fair Trade USA*, http://www.fairtrade.net/897.html, accessed on 20 May 2012.

FLO (2011o) *Monitoring the Scope and Benefits of Fairtrade, Third Edition*, www.fairtrade.net/impact_studies.html, accessed on 8 April 2012.

FLO (2011p) *Revised Fairtrade Prices and Trade Standards for Coffee: Main Changes*, http://coopcoffees.com/all_news/announcements-and-events/FLO%202011%20price%20changes.pdf, accessed on 12 December 2011.

FLO (2012a) *Fairtrade International Standards Committee Members*, April, http://www.fairtrade.net/setting_the_standards.html, accessed on 11 April 2012.

FLO (2012b) *Fairtrade Minimum Price and Fairtrade Premium Table*, Version 17/04/12, http://www.fairtrade.net/793.html, accessed on 20 May 2012.

FLO (2012c) *Producer Certification Fund*, http://www.fairtrade.net/producer_certification_fund.html, accessed on 12 Jan 2012.

FLO-Cert (2007a) 'Independence of FLO-CERT', *News*, 15 May, http://www.flo-cert.net/flo-cert/main.php?id=18, accessed on 17 March 2010.

FLO-Cert (2007b) *FLO-CERT GMBH: Certification in Fairtrade* (Promotional Brochure), http://www.flo-cert.net/flo-cert/main.php?lg=en, accessed on 18 July 2007.

FLO-Cert (2011) *Fee System Small Producer Organisation: Explanatory Document*, Version 23, Effective as of 22/12/2011, http://www.flo-cert.net/flo-cert/35.html, accessed on 22 December 2011.

FLO-Cert (2012a) *Our Goals*, http://www.flo-cert.net/flo-cert/30.html, accessed on 12 April 2012.

FLO-Cert (2012b) *Structure*, http://www.flo-cert.net/flo-cert/31.html, accessed on 12 April 2012.

FLO-Cert (2012c) *What We Are: About Us*, http://www.flo-cert.net/flo-cert/28. html, accessed on 12 April 2012.

FLO-Cert (2012d) *Application*, http://www.flo-cert.net/flo-cert/60.html, accessed on 26 May 2012.

FLO Standards Unit (2010) *Guideline for Estimating Costs of Sustainable Production*, www.fairtrade.net/793.html, accessed on 20 May 2012.

FLO Standards Unit (2012a) *Standard Operating Procedure: Development of Fairtrade Standards*, Approved 12 January 2012, http://www.fairtrade.net/setting_the_ standards.html, accessed on 11 April 12.

FLO Standards Unit (2012b) *Development of Fairtrade Standards – Short Summary*, http://www.fairtrade.net/setting_the_standards.html, accessed on 20 May 2012.

FLO Standards Unit (2012c) *Standard Operating Procedure: Development of Fairtrade Minimum Prices and Premiums*, Approved 12 January 2012, http://www. fairtrade.net/setting_the_standards.html, accessed on 11 April 2012.

FLO Standards Unit (2012d) *Standard Operating Procedure: Complaints Against Fairtrade Standards Setting*, Approved 12 January 2012, http://www.fairtrade. net/setting_the_standards.html, accessed on 11 April 2012.

Forstater, Maya, Jeannette Oelschaegel and Maria Sillanpää (2006) *What Assures Consumers?* An AccountAbility/National Consumer Council Report, July, http://www.accountability.org/about-us/publications/what-assures-2.html, accessed on 15 May 2012.

Frank, Andre Gunder (1966) 'The Development of Underdevelopment', in Rajani Kanth (ed.), *Paradigms in Economic Development: Classic Perspectives, Critiques, and Reflections* (New York: M. E. Sharpe), pp. 149–59.

Freer, Robert (1938) 'Fair Trade in Operation', *The Journal of Marketing*, 2, 4, pp. 303–8.

French, John (2002) 'From the Suites to the Streets: The Unexpected Re-emergence of the "Labour Question": 1994–1999', *Labour History*, 43, 3, pp. 285–305.

Gertler, Michael (2001) *Rural Co-operatives and Sustainable Development*, Centre for the Study of Co-operatives, University of Saskatchewan, Canada.

Giovannucci, Daniele and Freek Jan Koekoek (2003) *The State of Sustainable Coffee: A Study of Twelve Major Markets* (Colombia: ICO, IISD, UNCTAD, World Bank).

Gresser, Charis and Sophia Tickell (2002) *Mugged: Poverty in Your Coffee Cup* (Oxfam International), http://www.oxfamamerica.org/files/mugged-full-report.pdf, accessed on 28 May 2012.

Hamilton, Clive (2001) 'The Case for Fair Trade', *Journal of Australian Political Economy*, 48, pp. 60–71.

Hansen, Ursula and Ulf Schrader (1997) 'A Modern Model of Consumption for a Sustainable Society', *Journal of Consumer Policy*, 20, 4 (December), pp. 443–68.

Harrison, Rob, Terry Newholm and Deirdre Shaw (2005) 'Introduction', in Rob Harrison, Terry Newholm and Deirdre Shaw (eds), *The Ethical Consumer* (London: Sage Publications), pp. 1–8.

Harrison, Rob (2005) 'Pressure Groups, Campaigns and Consumers', in Rob Harrison, Terry Newholm and Deirdre Shaw (eds), *The Ethical Consumer* (London: Sage Publications), pp. 55–67.

Holme, Richard and Phil Watts (2000) *Corporate Social Responsibility: Making Good Business Sense*, World Business Council for Sustainable Development, http:// www.inggroup.com.au/pdf/csr2000.pdf, accessed on 23 August 2007.

Howse, Robert and Michael J. Trebilcock (1996) 'The Fair Trade-Free Trade Debate: Trade, Labor, and the Environment', *International Review of Law and Economics*, 16, 1, 61–79.

Howse, Robert and Michael J. Trebilcock (2002) *The Regulation of International Trade*, second edition (New York: Routledge).

Humphrey, Liz (2000) 'Which Way to Market? Exploring Opportunities for Marginalised Producers in Developing Countries to Supply Mainstream Commercial Companies in the UK', *Traidcraft Policy Unit Report Series No. 1* (April), http://www.traidcraft.co.uk/Resources/Traidcraft/Documents/PDF/tx/policy_which_way_to_market.pdf, accessed on 28 May 2012.

Hutchens, Anne (2009) *Changing Big Business: The Globalisation of the Fair Trade Movement* (Cheltenham: Edward Elgar).

ICA (2005) *Cooperative History*, www.ica.coop/coop/history.html, accessed on 8 Augugst 2007.

ICA (2005–2011) *Statement on the Co-operative Identity*, http://2012.coop/en/what-co-op/co-operative-identity-values-principles, accessed on 3 August 2012.

ICA (2007) *Cooperative Sectors*, www.ica.coop/coop/sectors.html, accessed on 8 April 2010.

ICA (2009) *Statistical Information on the Cooperative Movement*, last updated 2 October 2009, www.ica.coop/coop/statistics.html, 8 April 2010.

ICA (2010) *Current Cooperative Issues*, last updated 2 April 2010, www.ica.coop/coop/issues.html, accessed on 8 April 2010.

ICO (2005) *Governance*, http://www.ico.org/governance.asp, accessed on 25 October 2005.

ICO (2007a) *History*, http://www.ico.org/history.asp, accessed on 25 October 2005.

ICO (2007b) *Historical Data: ICO Indicator Prices – Monthly Averages*, http://www.ico.org/new_historical.asp, accessed on 25 September 2007.

ICO (2007c) *International Coffee Organisation – Historical Data: Exporting Data of Exporting Members (Calendar Years)*, http://www.ico.org/historical.asp, accessed on 25 September 2007.

ICO (2007d) *International Coffee Organisation – Historical Data: Supply Data of Exporting Members (Crop Years)*, http://www.ico.org/historical.asp, accessed on 25 September 2007.

ICO (2010a) *Indicator Prices, Annual and Monthly Averages: 1998 to 2010*, http://www.ico.org/prices/p2.htm, accessed on 26 April.

ICO (2010b) *Historical data: Prices to Growers*, http://www.ico.org/new_historical.asp, accessed on 2 April 2010.

ICO (2010c) *Historical Data: Retail Prices*, http://www.ico.org/new_historical.asp, accessed on 2 April 2010.

ICO (2010d) *Domestic Consumption – Crop Years*, http://www.ico.rog/new_historical.asp, accessed on 25 March 2010.

ICO (2012) *Historical Data*, http://www.ico.org/new_historical.asp?section=Statistics, accessed on 20 May 2012.

IFAT (2006) *Where did it all Begin?* http://www.ifat.org, accessed on 30 October 2006.

IFAT LA (2010) *Nuestros miembros*, http://www.ifat-la.org/miembros.php, accessed on 19 April 2010.

IFOAM (2009) *The Principles of Organic Agriculture*, http://www.ifoam.org/about_ifoam/principles/index.html, accessed on 28 August 2012.

IMF, World Bank and WTO (2003) Joint *Statement by Heads of IMF, World Bank and WTO*, Press Release No. 03/68, http://www.imf.org/external/np/sec/pr/2003/pr0368.htm, accessed on 16 May.

International Trade Centre (2011) *The Coffee Exporter's Guide, Third Edition*, www.intracen.org/The-Coffee-Exporters-Guide---Third-Edition/, accessed on 21 October 2012.

International Union of Food, Agriculture, Hotel, Restaurant, Catering, Tobacco and Allied Workers' Association (2002) *The WTO and the World Food System: A Trade Union Approach*, http://www.google.com.au/url?sa=t&rct=j&q=&esrc=s&source=web&cd=1&ved=0CCIQFjAA&url=http%3A%2F%2Fwww.iufdocuments.org%2Fwww%2Fdocuments%2Fwto%2Fwto-e.pdf&ei=oESLUJ32Oe2RiQeWuIGIBA&usg=AFQjCNE9p0MAdGJfUpNPJft5MEjqAM5RAg&cad=rja, accessed on 27 October 2012.

Ipsos MORI (2009a) *Brand Influencers: Opinion Leaders that Companies Cannot Afford to Ignore*, http://www.ipsos-mori.com/researchpublications/publications/1273/core-Summer-09-Brand-Influencers.aspx, accessed on 28 May 2012.

Ipsos MORI (2009b) 'Can You Hear Me?' Ipsos MORI Reputation Centre, http://www.ipsos-mori.com/researchpublications/publications/1287/Can-You-Hear-Me.aspx, accessed on 28 May 2012.

Irving, Sarah, Rob Harrison and Mary Rayner (2002) 'Ethical Consumerism – Democracy through the Wallet', *Journal of Research for Consumers*, 3, 3, http://www.jrconsumers.com/academic_articles/issue_3, accessed on 2 April 2012.

John, J. (2001) 'Fair Trade and Standard Setting: A Labor Rights Perspective', *Working USA*, 5, 1, pp. 64–9.

Khor, Martin (2005) *The Commodities Crisis and the Global Trade in Agriculture: Problems and Proposals*, Third World Network (TWN), May, http://www.twnside.org.sg/title2/par/td25.doc, accessed on 27 June 2006.

Kinnock, Neil (1994) 'Beyond Free Trade to Fair Trade', *California Management Review*, 36, 4, p. 124.

Kocken, Marlike (2006) 'Introduction', in Anja Osterhaus (ed.), *Business Unusual: Successes and Challenges of Fair Trade*, October (Brussels: FLO, IFAT, NEWS, EFTA), pp. 5–6.

Kornell, Sam (2007) 'Fair Trade™ or "Fairly Traded"?' *Coffee Talk*, XX, 5, May, pp. 12 and 14, http://www.coopcoffees.com/all_news/media/articles/fair-trade-or-fairly-traded-article, accessed on 9 August 2007.

Kravis, Irving (1968) "International Commodity Agreements to Promote Aid and Efficiency: The Case of Coffee", *Canadian Journal of Economics*, 1, 2, May, 295–317.

Krier, Jean-Marie (2005) *Fair Trade in Europe 2005: Facts and Figures on Fair Trade in 25 European countries* (Brussels: Fair Trade Advocacy Office).

Krier, Jean Marie (2008) *Fair Trade 2007: New Facts and Figures from an Ongoing Success Story*, A report on Fair Trade in 33 consumer countries, pp. 124–35, http://www.european-fair-trade-association.org/efta/DOC/FT-E-2007.pdf, accessed on 28 May 2012.

Lang, Tim and Yiannis Gabriel (2005) 'A Brief History of Consumer Activism', in Rob Harrison, Terry Newholm and Deirdre Shaw (eds), *The Ethical Consumer* (London: Sage Publications), pp. 39–53.

LeQuesne, Caroline (1996) *Reforming World Trade: The Social and Environmental Priorities* (Oxford: Oxfam Publications).

Lewin, Bryan, Daniele Giovannucci and Panayotis Varangis (2004) 'Coffee Markets: New Paradigms in Global Supply and Demand', *World Bank Agriculture and Rural Development Discussion Paper No. 3*, http://dx.doi.org/10.2139/ssrn.996111, accessed on 27 October 2012.

Linton, April, Cindy Chiayuan Liou and Kelly Ann Shaw (2004) 'A Taste of Trade Justice: Marketing Global Social Responsibility via Fair Trade Coffee', *Globalizations*, 1, 2, pp. 223–46.

Loureiro, Maria L. and Justus Lotade (2005) 'Do Fair Trade and Eco-labels in Coffee Wake Up the Consumer Conscience?' *Ecological Economics*, 53, 1, pp. 129–38.

Low, William and Eileen Davenport (2007) 'To boldly go ... exploring ethical spaces to re-politicise ethical consumption and fair trade', *Journal of Consumer Behaviour*, 6, 5, pp. 336–48.

Maseland, Robbert and Albert de Vaal (2002) 'How Fair is Fair Trade?' *De Economist*, 150, 3, pp. 251–72.

Mayo, Ed (2005) 'Foreword', in Rob Harrison, Terry Newholm and Deirdre Shaw (eds), *The Ethical Consumer* (London: Sage Publications), pp. xvii–xviii.

McDonagh, Pierre (2002) 'Communicative campaigns to effect anti-slavery and fair trade: The cases of Rugmark and Cafédirect', *European Journal of Marketing*, 5, 6, pp. 642–66.

Mendoza, Ronald and Chandrika Bahadur (2002) 'Toward Free and Fair Trade: A Global Public Good Perspective', *Challenge*, 45, 5, pp. 21–62.

Newholm, Terry and Deirdre Shaw (2007) 'Editorial – Studying the Ethical Consumer: A Review of Research', *Journal of Consumer Behaviour*, 6, 5, pp. 253–70.

Newman, Susan A. (2009) 'Financialization and Changes in the Social Relations along Commodity Chains: The Case of Coffee', *Review of Radical Political Economics*, 41, 4, pp. 539–59.

Nicholls, Alex and Charlotte Opal (2005) *Fair Trade: Market-Driven Ethical Consumption* (London: Sage Publications).

Office of the Cooperative Societies/Department of Trade and Industry (n.d.) *Revitalisation and Development of Cooperative Societies in PNG*, Boroko, Papua New Guinea (obtained in-country in December 2004).

Oxfam (2002) *Rigged Rules and Double Standards: Trade, Globalisation, and the Fight against Poverty* (Oxford: Oxfam International).

Oxfam (2006) *A Short History of Oxfam: Oxfam Today*, http://www.oxfam.uk/about_us/history/history9.htm, accessed on 11 October 2006.

Payer, Cheryl (1975) 'Coffee', in Cheryl Payer (ed.), *Commodity Trade of the Third World* (London: Macmillan), pp. 154–68.

Pérez Sueiro, Veronica (2006) 'The People Behind the Products', in FINE (ed.), *Business Unusual: Successes and Challenges of Fair Trade* (Brussels: FLO, IFAT, NEWS, EFTA), pp. 48–65.

Pierrot, Joost, Daniele Giovannucci and Alexander Kasterine (2010) *Trends in the Trade of Certified Coffee*, International Trade Centre, Geneva, http://papers.ssrn.com/sol3/papers.cfm?abstract_id=1736842, accessed on 17 February 2012.

Polaski, Sandra (2007) *Breaking the Doha Deadlock: Congress could Play a Pivotal Role*, Carnegie Endowment for International Peace, January, http://www.carnegieendowment.org/files/Polaski_final_formatted.pdf, accessed on 12 February 2008.

Ponte, Stefano (2001) 'The "Latte Revolution"? Winners and Losers in the Re-structuring of the Global Coffee Marketing Chain', *CDR Working Paper 01.3*, Centre for Development Research, July.

Ponte, Stefano (2004) 'Standards and Sustainability in the Coffee Sector: A Global Value Chain Approach', *Sustainable Commodity Initiative Paper*, Joint venture of the United Nations Conference on Trade and Development and the International Institute for Sustainable Development.

Raghavan, Chakravarthi (1997) 'A New Trade Order in a World of Disorder?' in Jo Marie Griesgraber and Bernhard G. Gunter (eds), *World Trade: Toward Fair and Free Trade in the Twenty-first Century* (Chicago, IL: Pluto Press), pp. 1–31.

Ramstad, Yngve (1987) 'Free Trade Versus Fair Trade: Import Barriers as a Problem of Reasonable Value', *Journal of Economic Issues*, 21, 1, pp. 5–32.

Ravenhill, John (1999) 'The Asia-Pacific', in Brian Hocking and Steven McGuire (eds), *Trade Politics: International, Domestic and Regional Perspectives* (London: Routledge) pp. 261–74.

Raynolds, Laura T. (2000) 'Re-Embedding Global Agriculture: The International Organic and Fair Trade Movements', *Agriculture and Human Values*, 17, 3, pp. 297–309.

Redfern, Andy and Paul Snedker (2002) 'Creating Market Opportunities for Small Enterprises: Experiences of the Fair Trade Movement', *Seed Working Paper No. 30*, International Labour Organisation.

Renard, Marie-Christine (2003) 'Fair Trade: Quality, Market and Conventions', *Journal of Rural Studies*, 19, 1, pp. 87–96.

Ricardo, David (1821) *On the Principles of Political Economy and Taxation*, Library of Economics and Liberty, http://www.econlib.org/library/Ricardo/ricP2a.html, accessed on 18 May 2012.

Rice, Paul (2012) 'Fair Trade USA: Why We Parted Ways with Fair Trade International', *Triple Pundit*, 11 January, http://www.triplepundit.com/2012/01/fair-trade-all-fair-trade-usa-plans-double-impact-2015/, accessed on 22 May 2012.

Riedl, Elisabeth (2009) 'Fairtrade: Evaluating Opportunities for Smallholder Coffee Growers in PNG', *Pacific Economic Bulletin*, 24, 2 (July), pp. 122–44.

Robbins, Peter (1995) *Commodities and their Markets: A Guide and Directory* (London: Kogan Page).

Robbins, Peter (2003) *Stolen Fruit: The Tropical Commodities Disaster* (London: Zed Books).

Robinson, Peter (2002) 'Bhagwati and Bello Square off over Free Trade', *Uncommon Knowledge*, Televised debate, 14 June, http://www.focusweb.org/publications/2003/jadish-walden-faceoff.htm, accessed on 15 April 2003.

Ronchi, Loraine (2002) *Monitoring Impact of Fairtrade Initiatives: A Case Study of Kuapa Kokoo and the Day Chocolate Company*, November, http://www.google.com.au/url?sa=t&rct=j&q=&esrc=s&source=web&cd=1&ved=0CCIQFjAA&url=http%3A%2F%2Fportals.wi.wur.nl%2Ffiles%2Fdocs%2Fppme%2FTwinMEKua paandDayA_5version.pdf&ei=pzuLUMvKN6egigfR2IDYAg&usg=AFQjCNFFD-fpJdjb2s64Qngg8lNz1n63hQ&cad=rja, accessed on 27 October 2012.

Sen, Amartya (1989) 'Development as Capabilities Expansion', *Journal of Development Planning*, 19, pp. 41–58.

Sen, Amartya (1999) *Development as Freedom* (Oxford: Oxford University Press).

Shiva, Vandana (1989) *Staying Alive: Women, Ecology and Development* (London: Zed Books).

Shreck, Aimee (2005) 'Resistance, Redistribution, and Power in the Fair Trade Banana Initiative', *Agriculture and Human Values*, 22, pp. 17–29.

Slob, Bart (2006) 'A Fair Share for Coffee Producers', in Anja Otserhaus (ed.), *Business Unusual: Successes and Challenges of Fair Trade* (Brussels: FLO, IFAT, NEWS, EFTA), pp. 122–39.

Smith, Adam [1789] 'An Inquiry into the Nature and Causes of the Wealth of Nations', in Edwin Cannan (ed.), *Library of Economics and Liberty*, Fifth edition (Methuen & Co, 1904), http://www.econlib.org/LIBRARY/Smith/smWN14. html, accessed on 28 May 2012.

Spich, Robert (1986)'Free Trade as Ideology: Fair Trade as Goal. Problems of an Ideological Approach in USA Trade Policy', *The International Trade Journal*, 1, 2 pp. 129–54.

Starbucks (2006) *Starbucks, Fair Trade, and Social Responsibility*, updated 7 March 2006, www.starbucks.com/aboutus/StarbucksAndFairTrade.pdf, accessed on 7 September 2007.

Starbucks (2005) C.A.F.E. Practices, www.starbucks.com/aboutus/sourcingcoffee. asp, accessed on 27 October 2012.

Starbucks (2010) *Responsibly Grown Coffee*, http://www.starbucks.com/responsibility/ sourcing/coffee, accessed on 22 April 2010.

Starr, Pip (direction, camera, editing) (n.d.) *The Okapa Connection: Organic and Fairtrade Coffee from the Purosa Region of Papua New Guinea*, 16.20 minutes, www.coffeeconnections.biz/purosa.htm, accessed on 9 July 2007.

Stoeckel, Andrew (1998) *World Agricultural Products Trade: Towards a Strategy for Australia*, Publication No. 98/127 (Canberra: Rural Industries Research and Development Corporation).

Stoeckel, Andrew and Brent Borrell (2001) *Preferential Trade and Developing Countries: Bad Aid, Bad Trade*, Publication No. 01/116 (Canberra: Rural Industries Research and Development Corporation).

Sukthankar, Ashwini and Scott Nova (2004) 'Human and Labor Rights Under the WTO', in Lori Wallach and Patrick Woodall (eds), *Whose Trade Organisation: A Comprehensive Guide to the WTO* (New Press, New York: Public Citizen), pp. 219–38.

Szentes, Tamás (2005) 'Development in the History of Economics', in Jomo K. S. and Eric S. Reinert (eds), *The Origins of Development Economics: How Schools of Economic Thought have Addressed Development* (New York: Zed Books), pp. 146–58.

Talbot, John M. (2004) *Grounds for Agreement: The Political Economy of the Coffee Commodity Chain* (Lanham, MD: Rowman and Littlefield).

Tallontire, Anne (2002) 'Challenges Facing Fair Trade: Which Way Now?' *Small Enterprise Development*, 13, 3, pp. 12–24.

Third World Network (2002) *Joint Statement of NGOs and Social Movements*, 26 January, http://www.twnside.org.sg/title/ngo2a.htm, accessed on 3 June 2008.

Traidcraft (2004) *Sell Fairly Traded Products*, http://www.traidcraft.co.uk/template2. asp?pageID=1497&fromID=1924, accessed on 24 October 2006.

Traidcraft (2005) *Traidcraft Purchasing Policy*, http://www.traidcraft.co.uk/about_ traidcraft/how_traidcraft_works/policies, accessed on 2 March 2010.

Traidcraft (2006) *Transforming Trade: Traidcraft's Strategy 2006–11*, http:// www. traidcraft.co.uk/temp/radF5891.pdf, accessed on 24 October 2006.

Traidcraft (2009) *Annual Review and Summary Social Accounts 2009*, http://www. traidcraft.co.uk/publications_and_resources/traidcraft_publications/annual- report. accessed on 2 March 2010.

Traidcraft (2012) *Impact and Performance Report for Traidcraft 2011–12: Incorporating the Financial Statements of Traidcraft Plc for the Year Ended 31 March 2012*, www.traidcraft.co.uk/about_traidcraft/financial_accounts.htm, accessed on 20 October 2012.

Traidcraft Exchange (2012) *Development Review 2012*, www.traidcraft.co.uk/publications_and_resources/traidcraft_publications/annual_reports.htm, accessed on 20 October 2012.

Traidcraft Foundation (2012) *The Traidcraft Foundation: Financial Statements for the Year Ended 31 March 2012*, www.traidcraft.co.uk/about_traidcraft/financial_accounts.htm, 22 October 2012.

Traidcraft Plc (2007) *Traidcraft Place: Financial Statements for the Year Ended 31 March 2007*, http://www.traidcraft.co.uk/NR/rdonlyres/8C87123A-CDB7-4B2F-805F-919D38C47784/0/finance_plc_accounts_2007.pdf, accessed on 17 October 2007.

TransFair Canada (2010) *Canadian Sales of (Labelled) Fair Trade Certified Products*, http://transfair.ca/sites/default/files/FTC%20Volumes%201997-2008.pdf, accessed on 18 March 2010.

TransFair USA (2004) *2003 TransFair USA Annual Report*, http://www.fairtradeusa.org/about-fair-trade-usa/financial-information, accessed on 27 October 2012. TransFair USA.

TransFair USA (2006) *2005 Fair Trade Coffee Facts and Figure*, http://www.transfairusa.org/content/Downloads/2004%20FT%20Facts%20and%20Figures.pdf, accessed on 7 February 2006.

TransFair USA (n.d.) Celebrating 10 Years: TransFairUSA 2008 Annual Report, http://tfusa.convio.net/site/MessageViewer?em_id=2621.0&dlv_id=6421, accessed on 22 April 2010.

Twin and Twin Trading (2011) *Annual Report 2010/11*, www.twin.org.uk/resources, accessed on 23 October 2012.

Twin and Twin Trading (2012) *Development through Trade: Twin Annual Review 2011–12*, www.twin.org.uk/resources, accessed on 23 October 2012.

Twin (2012) *Who we are*, http://www.twin.org.uk/who-we-are, accessed on 28 May 2012.

Twin and Twin Trading (2002) *Annual Report 01/02*, http://www.twin.org.uk/downloads/Twin_Annual_Report_0102.pdf, accessed on 24 October 2006.

Twin and Twin Trading (2005) *Fair Trade at the Crossroads: Annual Report 2004/05*, http://www.twin.org.uk/downloads/AnnualReport0405.pdf, accessed on 16 October 2007.

Udomkit, Nuntana and Adrian Winnett (2002) 'Fair Trade in Organic Rice: A Case Study from Thailand', *Small Enterprise Development*, 13, 3, pp. 45–53.

UNCTAD (2012) *About GSP*, http://www.unctad.org/Templates/Page.asp?intItemID=2309&lang=, accessed on 28 May 2012.

UNCTE (1948) *Final Act of the United Nations Conference on Trade and Employment: Havana Charter for an International Trade Organisation*, http://www.worldtradelaw.net/misc/havana.pdf, accessed on 12 April 2012.

United States Trade Representative (USTR) (2000) *What is the World Trade Organization (WTO)?* http://www.ustr.gov/wto/wtofact3.html, accessed on 15 August 2003.

Van den Berghe, Frederic (2006) 'Good Coffee, Bad Governance? The Legitimacy of FLO', *Center for Human Rights and Global Justice Working Paper*, 12,

NY School of Law, http://www.chrgj.org/publications/docs/wp/WPS_NYU_ CHRGJ_VandenBerghe.pdf, accessed on 20 May 2012.

Webb James Eall (1952) '"Fair Trade" Soaks the Consumer', *Changing Times*, 6, 8, p. 33.

Welford, Richard, Julia Meaton, and William Young (2003) 'Fair Trade as Strategy for International Competitiveness', *International Journal of Sustainable Development and World Ecology*, 10, 1, pp. 1–13.

WFTO (2009) *Market Access: Monitoring*, http://www.wfto.com/index. php?option=com_content&task=view&id=21&Itemid=302 accessed on 22 March 2010.

WFTO (2010a) *About Fair Trade: 10 Principles of Fair Trade*, http://www.wfto. com/index.php?option=com_content&task=view&id=2&Itemid=14, accessed on 24 May 2012.

WFTO (2010b) *WFTO Structure*, http://www.wfto.com/index.php?option=com_ content&task=view&id=5&Itemid=294, accessed on 19 April 2010.

WFTO (2011) Marks & Labels, *The WFTO Logo*, http://www.wfto.com/index.php? option=com_content&task=view&id=904&Itemid=310, accessed on 24 May 2012.

WFTO (2012a) *About WFTO: Who We Are*, http://www.wfto.com/*index*.php?option= com_content&task=view&id=890&Itemid=292, accessed on 28 May 2012.

WFTO (2012b) *Home: Market Access*, http://www.wfto.com/index.php?option= com_content&task=view&id=18&Itemid=49, accessed on 28 May 2012.

WFTO and FLO International (2009) *A Charter of Fair Trade Principles*, January, http://www.fairtrade.net/our_partners.html, accessed on 10 March 2010.

WFTO Asia (2010) *Asia Fair Trade Network*, http://www.wfto-asia.com/fair.trade. network.html, accessed on 19 April 2010.

WFTO Europe (2010) *WFTO Europe Members*, http://www.wfto-europe.org/lang-en/wfto-europe/europe-members.html, accessed on 19 April 2010.

WFTO Pacific (2010) *Members*, http://www.wfto-pacific.com/members/index. htm, accessed on 19 April 2010.

Wilkinson, Michael D. (1996), 'Lobbying for fair trade: Northern NGDOs, the European Community and the GATT Uruguay Round', *Third World Quarterly*, 17, 2 pp. 251–67.

Williamson, John (1990) 'What Washington Means by Policy Reform', in John Williamson (ed.), *Latin American Adjustment: How much has Happened?* (Washington D.C.: Peterson Institute for International Economics), pp. 5–20.

Wills, Carol (2006) 'Fair Trade: What's it all about', in FINE (ed.), *Business Unusual: Successes and Challenges of Fair Trade* (Brussels: FLO, IFAT, NEWS, EFTA), pp. 7–26.

World Bank (2003) *ICO and World Bank Address Coffee Crisis*, News Release No. 2003/310/S, 28 April, http://web.worldbank.org/WBSITE/EXTERNAL/NEWS/ 0,,contentMDK:20107928~menuPK:34463~pagePK:34370~piPK:34424~the SitePK:4607,00.html, accessed on 28 May 2012.

World Bank (2007) *World Development Report 2008: Agriculture for Development*, http://documents.worldbank.org/curated/en/home, accessed on 14 November 2008.

World Bank (2011) 'Gross National Income 2010, Atlas Method', *World Development Indicators Database*, 1 July, siteresources.worldbank.org/ DATASTATISTICS/Resources/GNI.pdf, accessed on 29 May 2012.

World Bank (2012a) Bananas, US, $/mt, current$, http://data.worldbank.org/indicator/BANANA_US?page=5, accessed on 28 May 2012.

World Bank (2012b) International Cocoa Organization Secretariat, http://data.worldbank.org/indicator/COCOA?display=map, accessed on 28 May 2012.

World Bank (2012c) International Coffee Organization, Thomson Reuters Datastream, Complete Coffee Coverage, http://data.worldbank.org/indicator/COFFEE_ARABIC/countries?display=map, accessed on 28 May 2012.

World Bank (2012d) Cotton Outlook, International Cotton Advisory Committee, Liverpool Cotton Services Ltd., http://data.worldbank.org/indicator/COTTON_A_INDX/countries?display=graph, accessed on 28 May 2012.

WTO (1994) *Agreement on Agriculture*, http://www.wto.org/english/docs_e/legal_e/14-ag.pdf, accessed on 12 April 2012.

WTO (2006) *Legal Texts: The WTO Agreements*, http://www.wto.org/English/docs_e/legal_e/ursum_e.htm, accessed on 4 May 2006.

WTO (2012) *Understanding the WTO: The Agreements: Agriculture: Fairer Markets for Farmers*, http://www.wto.org/english/thewto_e/whatis_e/tif_e/agrm3_e.htm, accessed on 20 May 2012 .

Young, Graham (2003) *Fair Trade's Influential Past and the Challenges of its Future*, King Baudouin Foundation, Brussels, http://www.traditionsfairtrade.com/class/documents/Youngbackgrounder-Eng.pdf, accessed on 28 May 2012.

Index